HURRICANE

INIKI and I

by

Bob Ward

Sheets & Halyards Publishing

ISBN: 0-9651219-0-9

Cover illustration by:
Dan Sutton, 663 Ahukini Place, Honolulu, HI 96825.

This story is a tribute to my friend Masa and to the memory of him and Nobuo.

My need to tell the story was based on local interest in Hurricane Iniki and the curiosity of friends about my sailing experiences.

ACKNOWLEDGEMENTS

Illona Rae Maki, Marva Kemp, Allen Walden and Chuck Carroll whose persistence and collaboration helped in the completion of this book.

Appreciation for encouragement from family and friends.

Bob Ward

Masa Hatanaka

Nobuo Saito

PREFACE

Hurricane Iniki and I is a descriptive account of my personal experiences of surviving a devasting storm during a fishing trip.

The record begins with the day my friend Masa warned Nobuo and I of an approaching hurricane as we headed for home base in Honolulu on the boat *Half Moon Bay*. There are flashes back to the development of my friendship with Masa, adventures on the sea, and my interest in boats. The story is enriched with glimpses of nostalgia and personal sentiments as memories of trips with Masa, my son's kidney disease, a broken marriage, alcoholism and my testimony of accepting Jesus Christ as my Savior are recalled.

My story returns to my fight for life during the hurricane of September 11, 1992 as I hung onto a floating tank while drifting off the southern coast of Kauai.

The story concludes with the descriptions of events leading up to my rescue, the people who played a role in my recovery and my discovery of inner peace.

CONTENTS

Hurricane Iniki and I - Bob Ward

Introduction

I was fifteen when I discovered the magic of alcohol: how it took away all of my inhibitions and made me feel like a man. Although short of stature, alcohol made me feel larger than I was. I was genetically blessed with a muscular body and never felt insecure at being five feet seven inches. My insecurity stemmed from being born with macular degeneration, an eye disease, which surfaced when I was in grammar school and is still progressing today. I was able to play Little League baseball, but had to give it up later when I couldn't follow the ball in Babe Ruth League.

I was able to play high school football and found it very gratifying. I even drove a car until I was twenty years old. My eye disease was progressing and I became paranoid of running over a child. I gave up my license to drive. My vision at that time was 20/200 in each eye.

I continued drinking through this time though it mostly took place on weekends and at parties. I was beginning to suspect that I had a drinking problem. I sometimes had bouts of depression. I drank and wallowed in self-pity because of my vision.

I was limited in the type of work I could do because of my eyesight. Hard labor was the kind of work I was capable of doing. I didn't mind this because I was strong and I like to sweat when I work. At the end of the day I enjoyed having some cold beer.

Once, while seeking work at a furniture movers company, I asked the foreman what the qualifications were for the job. He replied, "A size eighteen shirt and size two cap," The foreman later became my father-in-law.

I married at the age of twenty to Diana, the woman I would spend the next thirty years of my life with while raising our two children, Tiffany and Lance.

In 1965 we moved to Modesto from the Monterey Peninsula. Work was more plentiful in the Central Valley of California. There I found the job of my dreams. I became a lumper. A lumper is an independent laborer who contracts to load freight for truckers. We lumpers laughingly called ourselves "loading engineers". The qualifications were the same as for a furniture mover. I worked on Campbell Soup and Merchants Refrigeration docks and had to answer to no one. I could load as many or as few trucks as I wanted in a day and come and go as I pleased.

I was able to make a good living there. My wife continued her education and got a good job also. We almost lived happily ever after except that, between where I worked and my home, there were several saloons. The expression, "One is too many and a thousand is not enough" is true for me. I always stopped at the saloon to have only one beer. Inevitably I would get smashed.

There were times when I wouldn't drink if I had a project going on, or if I was coaching Little League. If I had some activity going with my family, such as vacations or some other activity, I would lay off the booze. I believe I was a functional alcoholic at that point, although I didn't know it. I always rationalized that, because I worked hard, I deserved a beer or two. This macho attitude, my self-centered thinking and immature emotional state were the three main factors that took me down.

Alcoholism is a progressive disease. It causes mental instability. If unchecked it can kill you. Death can result from diseases generated by drinking which, many times, can be disguised by alcohol.

Because of the ungoverned system of my job, it attracted all types of undesirables and transients. Virtually all the lumpers were drunks, dopers and junkies. This was not an environment where any

3

healthy person would want their son to follow in their foot steps, but for me this was an ideal job.

My marriage was falling apart. We saw a counselor who said that we couldn't be helped until I did something about my drinking. May 5, 1985, I found myself sitting on my garage floor with my pistol in my hand. I hated my life yet, at the same time, I was afraid to die. The only thing I knew for sure was I couldn't drink anymore. I'd lost a lot of weight, I was getting weaker and my liver was beginning to bother me. I knew that I had to get help or end it right there.

My son Lance was home convalescing from his kidney transplant. He had a rare kidney disease which destroyed both kidneys. The disease had possibly been caused by spinal meningitis which he had at age thirteen.

Lance and my brother, Michael, convinced me to go into an alcohol recovery unit for twenty eight days. The magic was gone; no more euphoria. Only pain and despair. I was an emotional, mental, physical and spiritual human wretch. The disease of alcoholism had finally caught up with me after twenty eight years of heavy drinking.

It was as if life had been stripped away to one raw nerve. The experience in recovery was like dying and being born all over again. I had to totally change my life to disassociate from all my prior acquaintances and modify all my routines. I literally had to begin to change my way of thinking. To an alcoholic change is a frightening proposition. It was the price of life. For me to drink was to die.

I plunged head long into Alcoholics Anonymous. I accepted the fact that I was an alcoholic and that my life was unmanageable. I began to build a new life.

The most profound experience in the recovery unit was during a class when the counselor explained the concept of the Johari window. The Johari window is a three-pained window. The first window is how we see ourselves. The second is how we think people see us; the third is how people actually see us. This was explained to me as an idea formulated by two psychologists named Joseph and Harry.

When I heard this explanation it was like someone had opened the top of my head and poured in the light. I was able to step out of myself and really look at myself objectively for the first time. I did not like what I saw. I saw how my negative behavior was being continually imposed upon other people. From that moment on I have been working to improve my behavior and work on my character defects. I even changed the way I walk. I'd had a cocky attitude which my walk had reflected.

I attended AA meetings for fifteen months and found myself falling into a rut. I began thinking more about my lifetime dream of sailing to islands with exotic names. This was the pipe dream I'd had all the years I sat on a bar stool.

My job had gone down the tubes because of the problems with the lumpers. The companies where we worked were bringing in their own freight handlers and we were being edged out. My children were grown and out on their own. My wife had secure employment. There was nothing to keep me from pursuing my dreams. I was forty-five years old and had good health except for my eyes. And I was sane and sober.

Iniki Strikes

Nine a.m., September 11, 1992: Masa let me sleep an extra hour as I had had the eight to midnight watch. We were all considerably tired after a full week of fishing. I preferred this watch. I then did not have to wake up from a deep sleep to stand watch. It made for a long day because we would start fishing at first light. As I climbed the four steps to the pilot house from the forecastle, Masa handed me the printout from the weather fax. He pointed with his finger and said, "A hurricane is coming." The fax showed three storms in line traveling west. He said the one in the middle, which was solid black on the printout, had just turned north. It was headed straight toward Kauai. We were just south of Kauai and directly in the storm's path. My first thought was to recall the typhoon I had experienced off Guam. I remembered how vicious the wind was the very first time I sailed with Masa. We were only on the fringe of that storm. We had caught winds of seventy-five to eighty knots. Even at that speed the horizontal watcr traveled in the wind and peppered our faces like buck shot. We were sailing up wind at that time and had to look forward; it was very uncomfortable. I also recalled that during the Guam typhoon it hit about 11 a.m. It was 7 p.m. by the time we were secured to a mooring in Agana Bay. During that time we were not able to consume food or drink. All hands had to be on deck to man the rigging.

Masa and Nobuo had already eaten. I grabbed a package of frozen waffles from the freezer and threw them into the microwave. Something told me to drink all the fluids I could. As I was eating, Masa began to radio the Coast Guard attempting to learn the status of the storm. We had a general idea of the size of the hurricane from the printout. It appeared to be sixty to seventy miles in diameter. We didn't know the speed it was traveling. Knowing the speed would give us an idea of whether or not we could run for cover toward a harbor, or possibly even run East by Northeast.

I drank what was left of the coffee and put on a fresh pot. Masa tried for several minutes but got no response from the Coast Guard in Honolulu. I thought it odd that there was no traffic on the radio. I finished cleaning my eating utensils, turned to Nobuo saying, "We need to secure everything on deck." As we went out the main hatch, I saw Masa pick up the cellular telephone. I noticed the sea looked like glass. There was not a whisper of wind or a ripple on the surface of the sea other than the wake left behind by our boat. It was still early in the day.

Even though we were through fishing and en route to our home base in Honolulu to Kewalo Basin, we hadn't stowed away our lines. By the time we had put our catch on ice the night before, it was already dark. We secured our outriggers from their holders and lashed them to the railing on top of the pilot house. The lures and miscellaneous fishing gear were put in the storage hold aft of the pilot house below deck. This was directly aft of the engine room. I was concerned about the fish hold hatch because it laid loose over the opening. The hatch had no hinges or any way to secure it. I grabbed some half inch line from the chain locker and laced it over the top of the hatch between the two hand rails on either side. I couldn't think of anything substantial to secure over the hatch at that time. I needed something to fill the two inch void between the hatch and the line. It would then put pressure on the hatch. There was absolutely nothing on hand. In retrospect I know it would have been futile anyway. The only other item on deck was the brine tank which was located aft of the fish hold on the lazerette, three steps down from the main deck. This six foot lazerette was an addition to the original boat plan. It was handy because it was only two feet above the water line with a tailgate like a pick-up truck. When larger fish were caught, it was easy to drag them aboard. The lazerette area was where most of our fishing was done.

Our brine tank was five feet in length and about eighteen inches by eighteen inches made of double-wall fiberglass with a bifold fiberglass lid. It was used to quick-chill the fish before we packed them in ice in our refrigerated fish hold. We used fresh water ice and salt water which, when combined, became colder than regular ice water. This process would keep fish fresh for days. We never touched our fish with our hands or let the fish touch the bulkheads. We packed each fish individually in ice to prevent any damage to them, and to insure a better price in the market.

Hawaii is a fresh fish market. The only treatment we gave the fish was to bleed the larger ones before putting them into the brine tank. This was done by cutting the large veins under the gills on each side of the head. Every fish is bid on individually at the auction where domestic and foreign buyers would purchase the fish. When our fish were displayed at the auction, they looked like they had just been caught.

Masa and I were always anxious when we went to the auction. We never knew the price our fish would bring. The morning after our return from a trip, the auction company would send a truck around to collect our fish about 4 a.m. At the auction house the fish would be rinsed, tagged, placed on pallets and put in rows. The auction usually began around 6 a.m.

Two years prior, when we bought the brine tank, I wished we had room on the boat for a larger one. A larger tank would not fit on the lazerette. Consequently I always had a fear of catching a very large fish. The ono (wahoo) we caught would just barely fit in the brine tank. Sometimes we would have to bend their tails in order for them to fit. We would straighten the tails when we packed them in ice. The average ono were five feet in length, and would grow thicker as they got older.

We bolted boards to the deck for stability around the base perimeter of the tank and screwed eyes to the boards. We then screwed eyes around the top perimeter of the tank. With the strongest twine we could buy, we laced the tank to the deck rolling the twine and using many strands. Then eyes were mounted on the perimeter boards near each end for bungee cords to secure the lid. Nobuo and I tied off the ends of all our fishing lines and made sure all the hydraulic reels were locked, that the hydraulic power was turned off on all seven reels.

I started forward to check our anchor which we had kept mounted on our bowsprit when I remembered that we had lost it after the first night when we tried to pull it up. We had anchored off the island of Niihau our first night out and had lost our anchor when we tried to retrieve it. We had snagged something and it had snapped the line which resulted in losing our hook, fifty feet of chain and two hundred fathoms of inch and a quarter line. The year before Masa and I had installed a new windlass and larger hydraulic pump. It was a powerful system capable of lifting many tons. Weight is easy to lift in the water until you reach the surface.

I don't know what it was we snagged, but it was extremely heavy. We took five wraps around the spool on the windlass, with two of us tailing and managed to pull up one hundred fathoms of line before it snapped. Sometimes I like to speculate about "the one that got away."

As Nobuo and I entered the cabin Masa was hanging up the cellular phone. He had spoken with his wife Valerie who had informed him that all ports were closed. We would have to ride out the storm. Valerie asked if we wanted to declare a state of emergency, but Masa said he didn't know how we could do that when there was no immediate problem. He also had learned that some harbors had been cordoned off.

I had never heard of harbors being closed prior to a storm. I was more than slightly disturbed when I heard they were closed. I always imagined that ports were a safe haven in times of storms. We would have had enough time to make Nawiliwili and secure before the storm. All Hawaiian ports are usually filled to capacity. I can almost understand the port authority ordering them closed. A boat as large as ours without a proper berth could do a lot of damage to docks and other boats if mooring lines were to break loose in a storm. However if the *Half Moon Bay* had been my boat, I would have taken her in regardless of what the Coast Guard or Port Authority had ordered. Although I was the paper skipper, I would never go against Masa's wishes to comply with the rules. He hated confrontations and didn't like to make waves.

I looked around to see if there were any loose objects and stowed away what I could find. Under normal circumstances, anything that wasn't nailed down would go flying. We usually kept everything stowed away because the *Half Moon Bay* was a roller. She would roll at least forty five degrees in each direction.

We turned on the TV. Usually we couldn't get any reception at sea because the rolling of the boat interfered with the frequency. The water was so calm the picture was perfect. We could receive one UHF channel which was giving the storm status. They now declared a state of emergency for Hawaii. They had begun evacuating the west coast regions of Oahu and were warning Kauai of the hurricane. Kauai was in the direct path of the storm and so were we. The announcer said we would get hit with winds of one hundred sixty five to one hundred eighty five knots which means winds in excess of two hundred miles per hour. I could not comprehend winds that strong, but remembering Guam in 1986 and eighty knot winds, I knew it would be hell.

From this time on very little was said. Every once in a while we would glance at each other with a questioning look but nobody spoke. We just waited. Gauging from my own thoughts we were all having our "what ifs." Unfortunately "what ifs" aren't usually what occur in reality. It gives temporary relief if you think you know what to do in certain situations. I kept running different scenarios through my head thinking what I might do in each situation. At sea it's usually the unexpected that gets you.

Something kept telling me to drink all the fluids I could; I continued drinking coffee. I found myself chain smoking because I knew once the storm hit it would be a while before I got another cigarette. Little did I know.

Although I had been in many storms the sea was never predictable and always acted a little

14

differently. The combination of the turbulent sea and the wind could become very treacherous.

All three of us had had our individual experiences with the sea. Nobuo had been working on a tall ship anchored somewhere in Florida when Hurricane Hugo struck. He had seen boats ripped from their moorings and slammed on the shore. He could only watch in terror, he said, as it happened. Fortunately the tall ship's mooring lines held fast and the ship he was on was spared.

Years before Masa had been in a typhoon where they had capsized. The keel was directly up and the boat wouldn't right herself. Masa had the crew, who were standing on the ceiling, jump from one side to the other to shift the weight. They did this for more than a minute before she rolled up. I believe that's one of those minutes that last a lifetime. This is one advantage of a sailboat over other types of boats. If you close her up, and her port holes and hatches hold, she will roll up and right herself.

I remember after the Guam experience the exhilarating feeling of having walked on the edge. How good it felt to be alive. Many people asked me if I was afraid. My reply was you don't have time to become afraid because you're so busy trying to survive. I don't recall any great surge of strength but am sure there must have been some adrenaline flow.

No one ever panicked nor did I ever see or hear fear from anyone. For this I am thankful. Panic can cause mistakes and mistakes at sea cause death.

Then there's always Murphy's Law. From all my experiences in life, it seems that Murphy's Law pertains more to boats than any other life endeavor I've experienced. It's probably due to the fact that you can't pull up to a marine store whenever you have a problem. Although most boats carry a multitude of spare parts, inevitably you end up having to jerry-rig something.

At all times I felt secure with Masa in any situation. He was constantly cool under fire and his foremost concern was for his crew and their safety. Masa's vast knowledge and experiences made him a great skipper. I always felt I would love to know even half of what he's forgotten. Although I can't honestly recall fear during this period of waiting, I know I felt a lot of anxiety. The unknown can cause more fear than can memories from past experiences.

The TV said to expect Iniki to hit Kauai between 1 and 4 p.m. She was moving faster than predicted. At about 11 a.m. the wind began to blow, the sea began to chop, the sun disappeared and the sky turned black.

I walked through the boat securing all the hatches and port holes, last of all, the main hatch which was constructed of heavy steel. It was a two-piece hatch with the top half being mostly glass framed by steel. Although we had air conditioning above the pilot house we always kept the hatch open for ventilation. In rough seas or at night we would close the bottom half of the door. When water came over the side it would slosh back and forth between the gunnels letting a lot of water into the cabin before flowing out the scuppers. The main hatch door had a thick rubber seal around the opening with huge hinges and four compression latches to make it water tight.

The pilot house was constructed helm to port with no seat. Masa had removed the seat. He thought that if someone was steering, and they became comfortable, they might go to sleep. This was easy to do, especially during the early morning watches. For me that was always the hardest time to stay awake. He preferred having the person stand during watch. About the only time we steered was entering or leaving a harbor, or while fishing. The boat had an excellent hydraulic autohelm.

To starboard was a bench seat with a chest-type freezer underneath where we kept our bait and also some food. This turned out to be a poor choice. We didn't have much alternative because the refrigerator-freezer compartment was small. We needed to always carry a two weeks supply of food. Once the freezer breaker tripped causing the squid

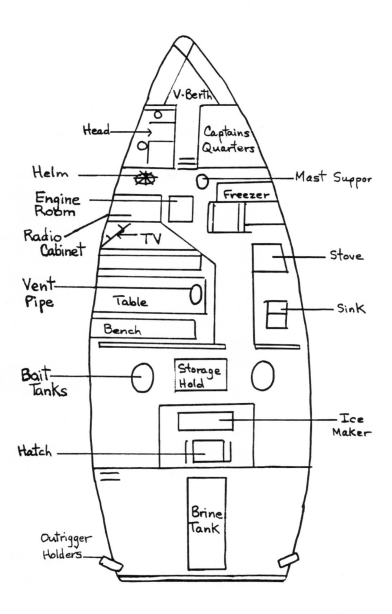

V·Berth

Captains Quarters

Head→

Helm

Mast Suppor

Freezer

Engine Room

Radio Cabinet

TV

Stove

Vent Pipe

Table

Sink

Bench

Bait Tanks

Storage Hold

Ice Maker

Hatch

Brine Tank

Outrigger Holders

bait to thaw. The smell permeated everything in the freezer including our waffles and hamburger patties. The hamburger we could disguise with onions. There wasn't much we could do with the waffles except hold our nose and wolf them down.

Across the dash from right to left was the chart table, plotter, radar and fish finder/depth sounder. Above the helm were the gauges for the engines and back to the right were our navigation instruments: Sat-Nav (Satellite Navigation), Loran C and G.P.S. (Global Positioning System). Pinpoint navigation is imperative in commercial fishing. You have to be able to return to the same areas where the fish are located.

With the three types of navigational equipment we could cross check one against the other. Sat-Nav is being phased out with only a few satellites remaining. The Loran navigation range is only good for a few hundred miles offshore. G.P.S. is accurate within a few meters, but the occasional military scrambling of it for defense reasons can put you off as much as a hundred meters. The down side of this is that, if you're traversing unfamiliar, charted reefs, fifty meters could sink your boat.

In the middle of the pilot house was the mast support and just to the left, between the mast support and helm, was the gangway to the forward cabins and head. The skipper's cabin was roomy with a double-sized bed. Across the companion way was the head with a full shower. Forward in the forecastle were four V-berths. Directly behind the helm was the radio cabinet which hid the helm from the salon. The radio cabinet was equipped with two single side band radios, a ham set and smaller VHF. Across from the radio cabinet was a full-sized refrigerator also placed into a partition so it wouldn't move. Between these was the engine room hatch which was constructed of four inch laminated wood like the rest of the pilot house deck.

The engine room was approximately eight by twelve feet with Detroit powered 471 Main and a Detroit 271 powering the twenty kilowatt generator. With all the engines, pumps, batteries and electrical boxes plus our tool boxes, every inch of space was accounted for. There was a narrow path on the starboard side. The main engine was a 471 which I always thought was small for that size boat yet it was considerably more fuel efficient than a 671. Aft of the refrigerator was a Genair stove and next to it was the sink ending at the main hatch. Across from these and on the port side was the settee, two bench seats facing forward and aft with table in between. Above the forward seat, mounted high on a shelf, was the television and video cassette recorder held down with half inch bungee cords. This arrangement

Masa and Nobuo

helped to separate the galley area from the pilot house. The entire cabin was encircled by glass windows three feet high stopping about four inches from the ceiling. The windows were all double thick safety glass. The aft bulkhead had two small windows about one foot square at each end of the short wall. The inside edge of the table was supported by an aluminum sailboat mast. It went through the ceiling of the cabin and came up from the engine room serving as a vent and support for the table. The mast was also something to grab when the boat was rolling.

The wind started building very fast now as was the sea. I threw out my last cigarette and shut the hatch. As I closed the top half of the hatch I realized how hot it was inside the cabin as I began to sweat profusely.

The boat began rolling and pitching without rhythm or regularity and the sea was coming from all directions. I felt like I was in a child's toy boat in a washing machine.

When the wind was seventy knots the EPIRB (emergency position indicating radio beacon), which was lashed to the outside of the aft bulkhead, broke free. It flew across the deck hitting the starboard gunnel and broke off the antenna. EPIRB is an emergency device that sends a signal to a satellite then back only to aircraft, like a tracking beacon.

There are several kinds and this particular type had a mercury switch which, when hung upside down, was off. It was weighted and when in the water it was self-righting thus began signaling automatically. When it hit the gunnel the antenna snapped off. We didn't know if it would still function. Nobuo stepped out to retrieve the EPIRB while I held the hatch from swinging which, at this time, was more deadly than the winds. The weight of this hatch could cause serious injury if turned loose with the violent pitching and rolling of the boat. I didn't see where Nobuo stowed the EPIRB. I was busy securing the hatch as Nobuo took his place next to Masa at the helm.

Objects were already starting to fly around the cabin. Some of them were unfamiliar objects, as I hadn't been on the boat for over a year. At one time I knew every item on the boat.

Masa yelled, "Wind going more to up-122 knots!" just moments before we got knocked down to starboard. We were in a deep trough laying at about a sixty degree angle. The water pressed against the cabin as if we were in a suction cup with water over half the top of the cabin. I was looking into green water and thinking of big fish with teeth. We were taking on water but we didn't know from where. The water started waist high at the front edge of the sink and reached to the cabin top. Masa saw the water and yelled, "Plug the sink!" He thought the flapper valve located about a foot above the water line was stuck open.

In a sailboat it's common practice to shut all ball cock valves located between the drains and the hull. This is not a common practice on fishing boats which do not heel like sailboats. All three of us were sailors and all of us knew that. Was it fear or distraction which prevented that from being done? Closing the ball cocks was one of the first things we should have done in a storm situation.

I put my hands over the sink drains but there was no resistance. It was then that I looked down at my feet and saw the water oozing in through the bottom of the hatch. Masa was at the helm and could not see how the water was coming in. All this time the engine was roaring and the heat was increasing in the cabin. At one point I recall seeing Masa stand up on the mast support holding onto the helm. I couldn't see Nobuo but I could hear him on the other side of the radio cabinet yelling to Masa who was standing next to him. It was then that I thought about taking the wheel. I gave up the idea because of the communication factor and opted to remain where I was. They spoke Japanese between the two of them. I was much stronger than either of them, but fast response was more important in this case and I didn't speak Japanese.

Suddenly the boat broke free like someone had pulled the plug on an electric magnet. The boat rolled to port about one hundred twenty degrees. I grabbed for the one inch sink rail. There wasn't enough to hold onto; my fingers just slipped off. I had just enough time to spin and put my hands out in front of me catching the end of the cushion on the settee. It was like falling into a hole although it happened in a split second and seemed like slow motion as I saw the cushion accordion up in front of me. I managed to roll my shoulder as I hit the port bulkhead and, if not for the cushion, I believe I would have broken my neck. If I'd landed two feet higher I might have gone right through the window.

As we rolled upright, I stood up, shaking my head and feeling somewhat groggy. While hanging onto the vent pipe, I saw Masa still struggling with the helm. We had two options: to run with or against the storm. The sea was so confused. I could see Masa was having trouble making any course while the compass was rotating back and forth. Not to mention the wheel which was being wrenched out of their hands and spinning like a propeller. I pictured the stern out of water and the rudder being hit by a wave. Meanwhile the ankle deep water ran forward to the gangway. There was virtually nothing I could do except stare in wonder. Everything seemed to come unraveled while I watched them struggle with the helm.

Nobuo sang out in Japanese, "Kaze hyaku yonju." (Wind one hundred forty knots). I knew he was referring to the wind speed. The boat went down again in the same position--about sixty degrees to starboard. We were again in a very deep trough. I could tell our stern was taking water and we were laying heavy aft. I could see green water covering half the hatch window. Although we were being pushed down by the wind, it felt more like we were being pulled by the force of the water. The air pressure made me feel like I was diving at two gravity. Once again the water was lying from the sink rail to the cabin top. Again I put my hands over the sink drains but could feel no resistance. There was a lot of debris floating in front of me including a pair of socks. I grabbed them and tried to plug the drains. I guess I did this out of the need to make any attempt to stop the entering of water. I knew I could do nothing about the water coming in the hatch.

At this moment something told me to stand up. As I did I stepped back with my left foot and stood facing the bow. A huge wave came crashing down on our port side. The wave impact fired an unknown object from the rail that ran along under the window. The object was about golf ball size. It passed just inches in front of my eyes in a blur. Then it penetrated about one foot of water and spider-webbed the inner sheet of the safety glass. I guess the pressure of the water outside kept it from blowing the entire window out. I ponder at God's will, as I write this. I believe if I hadn't moved at that instant, at the very least, that projectile would have knocked me unconscious or possibly worse.

This is when I saw the first sign of desperation from Masa. He grabbed a small drafting board that had been sloshing around the deck and pushed it onto the fractured glass. He held it there for several seconds then seeing the glass was holding, he turned loose of the board, turned around and exclaimed, "Oh! Going to hold." I thought this a bit absurd because, if the window had given way, all three of us could not have held the water back. Masa loved this boat. Things were coming apart and he was losing control of her.

Masa turned and made his way forward. As he reached Nobuo at the helm another wave came crashing down on us from the port side. At the same time, the television fell off its pedestal and was hanging by its cord. I was surprised the cord held when the TV fell. Masa then yelled, "Bob--the TV!" as I was moving toward the TV which I took to mean "save the TV." I was standing on the face of the lower sink cabinet. I stretched for the TV as it was swinging up and down and could just touch it with my fingertips. The only way I could reach it would be to stand on the one inch lip at the end of the settee. The boat was surging and tossing about one foot side to side very quickly as was the TV. I would need both hands to grab it. I thought about the last time the boat righted herself and I backed off. The TV went crashing into the cabinet as another wave hit our port side. I could see that it was enough to fill the trough and we rolled upright. I slid the TV along the deck, climbed down the gangway, and said to Masa, "Sorry about the TV." He looked a little disapprovingly, but I thought my hide was worth more than a $200. television. I then turned, grabbed the TV and stowed it on the deck between the V-berths in the bow.

Everything was in disarray in the forecastle. I thought about grabbing a T-shirt because I felt that we were going to eventually have to abandon ship. But I was nervous about being below. As I scampered up the gangway I was amazed at how dry it was in the forecastle when everything else in the rest of the boat was so wet. I guess the forecastle was dry because, unknown to us at the time, she was taking water from the stern thus causing her to lay heavy aft. I returned to my position aft in the pilot house and helplessly watched as Nobuo and Masa struggled with the helm. They were trying to make some kind of course and occasionally having the wheel ripped from their grasp as it spun freely.

I have no idea how long the intervals were that we were upright or knocked down. As I look back, it seems like a very short time. I knew it was at least two hours between the time the storm hit, until the third time we were knocked down. We resumed our prior position at sixty degrees starboard. It was at this time I knew the boat was going to sink. Masa looked at me and I asked him, "Where are the life jackets?" He shook his head and said, "Don't have." I felt a little numb but also reassured knowing there was a life raft on the top deck of the pilot house.

The engine died. Masa opened the engine room hatch, went down and restarted the engine. I turned to look aft only to see green water through the main hatch. This meant the whole stern was under water to amidships. As Masa came up from the engine room I could only see dark sky through the forward pilot house windows. Water was rushing past me in a stream in the "V" between the deck and the sink cabinet. It was about a foot wide, maybe six to eight inches deep and going directly into the engine room. I couldn't believe water could come through that hatch with all that pressure against it. Possibly the door jam was originally warped allowing the water to flow through a minute crack. Suddenly the bow dropped. The boat became level but was still listing sixty degrees to starboard. There must've been a forward surge of water through the bilge and into the engine room and the forecastle to make the boat level out. Then the engine died.

Masa closed the engine room hatch. In one last act of desperation he told me to get a pan so we could try to bail. As I reached through the water into the cabinet for a pan, Nobuo climbed on the console in front of the helm. I passed the pot of water to Masa who passed it to Nobuo. Nobuo opened the small hatch overhead but the wind was so fierce he couldn't maneuver the pan into position to spill it out and gave up. I knew it was futile before we tried, but I could tell Masa was desperate. He loved this boat. He saw her dying and he was helpless.

When Nobuo opened the hatch to bail out water, I could hear the wind whistling a very loud sound as it blew across the open hatch. I turned and faced Masa with my thumb pointed up indicating the time to abandon ship had come. He only nodded. As I look back I'm surprised how little was said through the whole ordeal.

Nobuo then produced the EPIRB from the console behind the plotter and handed it to me. Knowing I would need two hands, I slid my left hand and forearm between the EPIRB and wires which were maybe ten coils that had held it to the bulkhead. As Nobuo opened the small pilot house hatch above the freezer he began climbing out. Masa went to the sink cabinet and grabbed the French knife. I climbed out second, was halfway out and had just grabbed the rail overhead when a wave broke over the boat. It ripped the EPIRB off my arm which then disappeared into the sea.

Masa yelled "Hurry!" as I pulled myself the rest of the way out. Masa scrambled out very quickly. We were all standing on the pilot house top rail and holding onto lines and any other objects on the deck. I was forward, Masa in the middle and Nobuo aft. The hatch was still open and I got a strong whiff of ammonia. I asked Masa what it was. He said he didn't smell anything. I guess he was up wind of it. I think the smell of ammonia came from a combination of sea water and sulfuric acid as the batteries became submerged in water.

I looked at the cradle where the canister of our six man life raft had been. It was empty! These life rafts are designed so that when submerged they automatically inflate breaking the stainless steel bands that hold them in the canister and cradle. It has a hundred foot painter that keeps it attached to the cradle. Either the winds or waves or both had ripped the raft away, snapping the line. I asked, "Where's the raft?" Masa pointed toward the horizon and said "There!" I could not see it.

I got a hollow and hopeless feeling in the pit of my stomach. As I look back I think the life raft would probably have been another death trap in the violent seas of Iniki. With the thirty and forty foot waves breaking over us, we could have become entangled in the raft upside down and drowned. I'm sure the raft would have tumbled with us in it.

Then the *Half Moon Bay* laid down. The seventy foot mast was lying flat on the water. It was like she had taken her last breath.

I noticed the wind had stopped blowing. Masa dove down with the knife to cut loose the two life jackets that were tied to the cradle and were now several feet under water. I saw the two life jackets when I climbed out of the hatch. I remembered having asked Masa where the life jackets were. I have to think he had meant there were none inside the boat. Maybe he had forgotten about the two on the deck. Who knows what was going on in his mind. The sea was still angry and was beating Masa against the deck. He came up empty-handed. He also had lost the knife.

Nobuo yelled something and started walking out on the mast while hanging onto the main shroud; Masa followed him. I didn't know what they were doing and began to follow also. I wanted to help in any way I could to ensure our survival. I felt an overwhelming stab of fear for the first time. I didn't want to be left alone. I saw Nobuo going to retrieve a Styrofoam surfboard about five foot in length that had been tied to the top deck next to the cradle. When I saw what they were doing, I back-tracked and stepped aft to allow more room for them. Masa no sooner returned when he pointed and yelled, "Bob! The brine tank" It was bobbing about fifty feet off the stern. I was astonished at how a wave could knock this tank off the deck which we'd had so firmly secured. I still had my foul weather boots on. I kept my boots rolled half-way down when we weren't fishing. This made them easy to pull on and off. I kicked them off and dove into the water. I had only taken a few strokes when I thought about my white socks attracting sharks. I hooked my big toe into the elastic pulling off one then the other as I stroked with my arms.

I reached the brine tank quickly and was glad that I'd taken the time the night before to scrub it out. Any blood in the tank would have surely attracted sharks. With my fear of swimming in the ocean and being a weak swimmer as well, I immediately tried to climb on top of the tank. It only rolled away from under me. There were some strings but they pulled loose when I grabbed hold of them. I found the best way to hang on was to pull the end of the tank against my chest with the open side down. I held onto the open edge under water with my left hand and laid my right arm pit on the bottom corner with my arm extended along the long edge.

By this time I had drifted to the masthead and Masa and Nobuo joined me in the water. The sea had calmed considerably. Nobuo was lying on the surfboard while Masa had one arm across his back and one over the brine tank. We drifted around toward the bow, but away from the boat. We were being pushed away by the current. I didn't see it happen nor do I think they did because of Masa's response which was "Oh!" The boat had righted herself with just the top of the pilot house deck and the mast visible. We started kicking and trying to maneuver the tank to the boat, but it wouldn't cut the water. They spoke in Japanese and Nobuo said, "Wait here" as they struck out for the boat. I assumed they were going back for the life jackets tied to the deck. The wind was building again and the sea was starting to churn. I had thought the storm had passed, but now I realized we were in the eye. We now had the second half of the storm to reckon with.

Adventures at Sea

August 1986:   I was in Honolulu for my daughter Tiffany's wedding. She was going to marry Robert Shiraishi, a local boy.

I saw a "crew wanted" slip on the bulletin board at Ala Wai Marina. I inquired and met Masa. He was looking for crew to deliver the *Marishiten*, a fifty six foot titanium racing sloop to Guam, and then either to New Zealand or Yokohama. Either way I didn't care.   I was simply eager to gain further sailing knowledge and experience.

I had just returned to California in July from a round-trip sail to Victoria British Columbia. It had been a cold, wet sail but good experience. We'd had a lot of bad weather with winds of forty to forty five knots.

We were about one hundred sixty miles out heading south en route to San Francisco when the trip became exciting. We lost our main shroud. We then pulled down all our canvas and started motoring toward the nearest port, Fort Bragg, California.

About sixty miles west of Fort Bragg we ran out of fuel. We tried calling the Coast Guard for several hours, but didn't get any response. We turned on our EPIRB.

About 9 a.m. the next morning, we were lying dead in the water with a Liberian freighter bearing down on us. For fifteen minutes we watched her approaching as we constantly were radioing her and getting no response. She was on a collision course with us. Finally a Coast Guard helicopter responded to our EPIRB. The helicopter hovered above the freighter and they changed course just in time. We were about one hundred meters from becoming minced meat. Nowadays it seems that these ships compute and plot their course. Everything is turned on automatic and everyone on board goes to sleep.

When I first met Masa at the Ala Wai Marina I took an instant liking to him, as I found most people did. The first time I saw Masa (Masato) Hatanaka, he was sitting in the cockpit of the *Marishiten* with his two crewmen, Takeo and Hidei. I was taken back by how dark he was from the sun. He was about five feet six inches, slight of build. His hair was long, maybe three or four inches below the ears. He wore a short goatee. Someone made the comment once that I was a Haole (Caucasian) version of Masa. Except for the eyes we might have passed for brothers.

I was nervous that Masa wouldn't pick me as one of the two crewmen he needed. I had only one cruise under my belt which was San Francisco to Victoria and back to Fort Bragg. Later I learned what Masa already knew; experience wasn't as important as compatibility and willingness to follow orders. Besides Masa always knew what everyone was doing. He had an easy way about him, but he was direct and he ran a fairly tight ship. Masa was usually upbeat and wore a little grin on his face. He always looked somewhat mischievous to me, rather like the little boy that gets caught with his hand in the cookie jar.

Masa was constantly on the move, never tiring, always busy, invariably fixing something or studying some manual or electronic equipment. Masa was thrifty but I think one of his favorite activities was to go to swap meets and marine salvage stores. Our favorite store was the marine store located on Sand Island Road in Honolulu. We called it the "gomi" store which in Japanese means garbage. Come to think of it, we jokingly called everything "gomi". Masa would buy something broken for pennies on the dollar, take it home and fix it. He knew the good from the junk. I think he got as much enjoyment from that as a gambler hitting Black Jack. I was always amazed at how much he could eat. I out-weighed him at least thirty pounds. It goes without saying, he burned the calories.

I would become tickled by him when we went somewhere His short legs would fly; I would have to hustle to keep up. Especially in airports he would get a little irritated when I wouldn't keep up.

I always enjoyed working on things with Masa. It was kind of like we were Mutt and Jeff. He was the brains and I the brawn. I liked the way he would approach a problem. I'd bet that he's torn more than one clock apart. Probably the nicest compliment he paid me was when he told me my fingers were stubby on the end like his. I believe he meant that this came from doing hard work with our hands.

September 5, 1986, we set sail for Guam. Masa, Takeo, Hidei, myself and Mike, a twenty three year old from Southern California set sail on the *Marishiten*. It was a mellow trip until six days out when we entered the doldrums. Mike became "antsy" and began asking, "When are we going to see land?" I tried to console him by saying all sailors experience doldrums sometime or another, but it didn't seem to help. At times the wind became

Hulling out the *Marishiten* for shipment

Masa & Bob

so light that we were unable to steer the boat. It would just drift uncontrollably in circles. We had to begin motoring.

Masa used what is called the "Swedish system" for watches. A crew of five is ideal. It works out where each member of the crew is on watch for two hours and off for eight hours. With this system watch is always rotating and you're not stuck on the same watch continually.

Everyone chipped in with the cooking and cleaning. We had a lot of free time. I'd brought a Walkman and tapes and kept a journal as I did on all cruises. We would open up all the hatches and lie around on the sail bags in the forecastle. I would try to learn Japanese from Hidei and Takeo. They would work on their English and "talk story" with each other in English which was better than my Japanese.

The highlights of the days were sunsets. I had never seen sunsets like these. The colors were brilliant--from yellow, orange and red to lavender. We took photos with good cameras, but still couldn't capture all the radiant shades of sunset colors. Each evening after dinner everyone would come on deck for the color show.

I don't recall one stormy day on the trip. During the day there were huge billowy clouds 360 degrees around us. They looked like white, fluffy monsters stretching from the horizon hundreds of feet into the sky. Although they were always there we never reached them. Almost every day one dark cloud would pass overhead and we would grab our shampoo and soap. It would last only a minute or so, but by standing under the main sail, it was like a torrential down pour. It was very refreshing and helped to cool our temperatures for a while. The water, the air and our bodies all felt the same temperature. Sometimes at night we could see lightening spreading across the western sky far off in the distance. We would wait expectantly for the thunder which never came.

Our refrigeration had ceased to function after the first week. All food and drink items, except for what we cooked, were at room temperature. I'm not partial to milk shakes, but I found myself craving vanilla milk shakes.

There is no chain of life in the middle of the ocean, at least not at the surface. There wasn't even any phosphorous light made by the wake of the boat which is always seen near land at night.

Masa told me that the average depth of the Pacific Ocean is three miles. It makes me wonder what could be down there. The water out in the middle is such a pale blue green you can see a long, long way down.

At night the stars were so bright I could pick one of many to steer by regardless of our course. I always resented the moon coming up. It would be so bright it would blur out the more distant stars forcing me to sometimes use the compass. When there is no overcast, the stars alone shed enough light to see for miles. Just a partial moon makes it seem as bright as day. I've been told that most boats being run over by ships usually get it from the stern. Whoever is on watch forgot to look behind them.

One night at the helm, I looked back to see rays of light illuminating across the horizon. I grabbed the binoculars and watched them for a minute. The lights grew very fast. It looked like a huge cruise ship was bearing down on us. I yelled for Masa. He stuck his head out of the hatch, watched it for a minute, said "moon" and disappeared below. I kept watching it. Soon it transposed and appeared as an island. When sailing past a populated island below the horizon at night, the island puts off a glow similar to this stage of the moon rising. After a few minutes I could see the rim of the moon breaking over the horizon. I am thankful that God blessed me with the opportunity to see such things.

We should have made Guam in eighteen days, but with the light winds it took twenty five days. On the 20th day we ran out of fuel. The fuel tank was a flat tank that laid in the bilge above the keel. We didn't have a fuel gauge. This would not have been a problem except we cooked by electricity from our generator. We ate cold food from that point on. We tried various ways to heat water--even wrapping black plastic around a gallon jar of water. We hoped it would work sort of like a solar blanket. We found it ineffective. It's amazing the different things we tried when we didn't have the proper tools.

October 1st: I was on watch; it was about 11 a.m. when it started to blow. There were two typhoons on our weather fax. We had monitored the typhoons throughout our trip. Both were traveling about the same speed we were. The only difference between a hurricane and a typhoon is the location on the globe. In the western hemisphere they're referred to as a hurricane while in the eastern hemisphere they're considered a typhoon.

One typhoon stayed five days ahead of us and turned north before reaching Guam and harmlessly continued on its way. The other typhoon was south and ran parallel to us. It turned north and hit us just as we sighted land. This was the first time I had been at the helm in this heavy of a blow, and in this type of boat. For fifty-six feet she weighed only ten tons and was very fast. She began heeling more and more. I yelled to Masa who was at the chart table below. He yelled back, "Hold your course." Soon the stanchions were cutting water. Then the water was knee high from the edge of the cockpit and we were going like hell.

The *Marishiten* was not equipped with cruising sails. There were no reef points on the main sail and our smallest foresail was a working jib. It was now blowing seventy knots. We were on the So. East side of Guam and had to go to the N. West side of the island for cover in Agana Bay.

We proceeded North up the eastern side of the island, turned West along the end of the island then South. All the time we were getting hit quite hard. At the time I thought we were going to ride out the storm at sea, but as we neared the opening of the harbor, I heard someone ask if we were going in. I saw Masa nod yes. I looked at him questioningly. He looked directly into my eyes and calmly said, "No problem."

When we went through the opening of the small horseshoe-shaped bay, I saw rocks around the circumference of the bay and became very apprehensive. It was a small bay with a short stretch of beach directly ahead from the opening. My first thought was no motor, winds at eighty knots and under full sail. At this point I stopped thinking, became wide-eyed and waited for orders. We came flying in with the wind on our starboard beam. Just as calmly as if we were entering a slip, Masa turned up into the wind, we slid onto a mooring buoy and stopped. As we slid backward from the force of the wind another crewman and I dropped the sails. One crewman snagged the mooring buoy while another laid over the bow and fed lines directly through the buoy eye.

Racing boats, like the *Marishiten*, don't have heavy mooring cleats. We ran several sheets back and forth through the buoy and around the mast a dozen wraps. Only one line snapped. It had to be under tremendous pressure to snap that five-eighth inch sailbraid.

It was now 7 p.m. and getting dark. We had everything secured when I took time to look around. Waves were crashing on the shore and bouncing about fifty feet in the air. I was surprised at how small the harbor was. I would guess we were no more than one hundred feet from the nearest rocks.

I asked where all the boats were. Masa said they had all gone up the small channel to a protected harbor. Even if we had fuel we couldn't go because it was a shallow channel. The *Marishiten* had a ten foot draft. The channel was only five feet deep at low tide. The boat was still violently pitching and rolling. I felt that as long as the mooring held we and this two million dollar boat were safe. I started going over the events of the day and thought about how Masa had stood at the helm with the wind and water beating his face. I was impressed at how tough this little guy was. I thought to myself I'll sail anywhere with this guy!

It was 11 a.m. the next morning before the storm passed. We were about to go ashore. Mike blew a golden opportunity when early in the morning he became irrational. He started pounding on the aft rail with a dingy oar and yelling, "I want off this damn boat!" He was acting ridiculous considering how the waves were breaking on the shore. His behavior was embarrassing to me. We were all anxious to stretch our legs after twenty five days at sea. Without hesitation, when it was time to go ashore, Masa told Mike to take his gear. I felt sad for him because there were good things to come and he was going to miss out. We were now short-handed. We picked up another crew member, Gavin, for the remainder of the journey to Yokohama. I didn't get to know Gavin that well. He was comical and quite a ladies man.

Masa offered Mike a ticket back to Honolulu but he declined. During the storm a container full of beer had broken loose from a ship. Hundreds of cans of beer washed ashore. Mike was taken aboard by two brothers who had collected vast quantities of this cargo. I guess they partied vigorously. I hope Mike fares well.

We stayed in Guam for about two weeks except for a three day sail to and from Saipan. There we met the Japanese owner of the *Marishiten* who stayed a few days then flew back to Japan. From what I understood, the owner was contemplating sending the boat to New Zealand, to have the interior fitted out and to put her up for sale. I think he opted to keep and race her one more year in the next Long Beach to Honolulu TransPac race. These racing boats are nothing more than an outer shell. The lighter the boat the more speed obtained.

Of all the Marianas Islands I found Saipan to be the prettiest. I visited the Blue Grotto at night. Because of poor visibility I couldn't see it that well. The Blue Grotto is where the Japanese made their last stand on the island of Saipan. Most of the population of Saipan are Chimoro people. I found them to be a friendly and attractive-looking people.

I watched one of the natives prepare a chew of beetle nut by wrapping the nut and piece of lye with a leaf. I chewed the beetle nut and spit red. It had a bit of bitter taste, not distasteful. It made me feel somewhat mellow. Many of the natives on Saipan chew beetle nut. I was told that it was very addictive. I suppose if I had chewed more of it I could have acquired a taste for it. We spent one night at the home of a friend of Masa's on Saipan.

Our host carried a small paper bag full of beetle nut with him in his car.

Someday I would like to return to further explore the island and to see the Blue Grotto in the daytime. I saw my first land crab as we were leaving the Blue Grotto. They're called coconut crabs on Saipan. I understand they're delectable though I did not get to taste one. We then sailed back to Guam where we stayed for another week.

We set sail for Chichijima, five days from Guam with fair winds. On the way we passed Maug, the last island in the Marianas chain. Guam spelled backwards. Maug is a barren, steep-sided, cylindrical-shaped, volcanic peak. It has an opening on its south side into which we could have sailed. It looked like a good storm haven for a boat--if there had been a way to run mooring lines.

We also passed Iwojima. I asked Masa if we could stop for a short time. He said it was military owned and off limits.

Back in the early whaling days, Americans called Chichijima "Bonin Island." Whalers would take their catch there to process them. Chichijima is a popular site for Japanese tourists. It has a ferry that travels to Tokyo and back, about a forty hour trip one-way. It arrives approximately once a week and provides fresh fruit and vegetables and other supplies for the island. Chichijima is a beautiful island with good diving and fishing.

Chichijima means "Mother Island". There are several islands in the group, the remainder of which are primarily uninhabited. The islands are small and composed of very steep, mountainous peaks. We explored the island and saw World War II bunkers and a small, sunken freighter lying in the bay. There were some scars left from World War II. It appeared that the main source of income for island residents is fishing and tourism--mostly tourism though I did see a marine lab.

I was introduced to some Japanese fishermen whom Masa knew. They'd caught a baby whale in their nets. The whale had drowned before they could free it. I felt somewhat ashamed of the idea of eating whale--especially baby whale--but I knew I'd never have this encounter again. The meat had a similar appearance to liver and a taste between beef and liver. I don't know which part of the whale was given to us. We took it back to our boat, fried it and found it to be quite tasty.

We made one more stop after Chichijima while en route to Yokohama. Four days later we sailed past Pinnacle Rock, a narrow, weather-worn, jagged peak approximately fifty feet high protruding from the water and totally out of context with the sea. It looked like Neptune's little finger.

We sighted Hachijojima shortly after, a clean beautiful small island about one day sail from Honshu. We stopped for a couple hours to sightsee and to pick up some fuel for the boat. I asked Masa why all of the islands names ended in "jima". He said "jima" means island. I just said "oh" and felt like a fool.

Hachijojima is a steep, mountainous island with a well-protected harbor on its eastern side. There were several fishing boats and a few pleasure craft in the harbor. Hachijojima was like I had always imagined Japan to be. It had well-manicured yards and gardens with bonsai trees and plants. There was no litter to be seen anywhere. Hachijojima spoiled me for the reality of highly industrialized and over-populated Japan.

My last watch: At 11 p.m. we had fair winds with long swells as we were entering Tokyo Bay. We were doing seventeen knots and the boat's hull was humming. Needless to say, I was really excited, but Masa told me the boat had done better than twenty before.

Masa and I became friends. We had shared many thoughts although communication was sometimes a problem. We somehow were able to understand one another in most instances.

I stayed at Masa's home in Kawasaki for several weeks. I became well-acquainted with

Masa's mother, his two sons and his grandchild by his youngest son--all of whom made me feel welcome and comfortable. His mother and sister were excellent cooks. They kept us well fed. I believe that I have eaten every kind of seafood known to mankind. Masa and I always did a lot of traveling and we often ate in restaurants. My favorite ones were soba restaurants who specialized in soba noodles. My preference was "tendon" which is butterfly, tempura shrimp over rice with a special sauce.

While I was at Masa's home in Kawasaki, I expressed to him that I was considering building a boat. I became more inspired being in Masa's yard with the four boats and boat molds he had made. Masa was a highly respected and well-known boat builder in Japan who had designed and built several boats. I had been considering building a boat for some time. Seeing Masa's work inspired me to go forth with my project. Masa asked me what size boat I was thinking of building. I said "Around forty feet." He responded with, "Take that engine." He pointed to an Izusu Diesel Marine sitting in the corner of his shop. Masa answered many questions and gave me invaluable tips about boat building. He cleared up a lot of my doubts and questions about taking on such a task.

The owner of the *Marishiten* was most hospitable. He took the crew many places: restaurants and night spots. The highlight of this journey came near the end of my stay in Japan when the owner took the crew to Korea for an extended weekend. We stayed at the General Walker Hotel in Inchon, approximately forty minutes west of Seoul. We were each given a million won with which to gamble. The hotel had a casino on an upper floor. The food was fantastic--anything could be had at any time. All expenses were paid. I won big at the Black Jack tables. One day I took a taxi into Seoul to sightsee and to spend some of my winnings on jewelry and clothes--gifts for friends and family.

Masa had said now much he liked El Camino pickups. I had spoken with my wife in California who had told me she had blown the engine in my El Camino and had bought a new truck. When I returned home for Christmas I bought a rebuilt engine and installed it in the El Camino. I painted it and stored it until Masa called for it. He didn't know I had done the body work and painted the El Camino and was surprised and pleased when he saw it. Meanwhile Masa had shipped the Izusu engine for the boat to me in California. I then began construction on my forty foot boat.

In 1989 Masa bought the *Half Moon Bay* who's name was the *Feresa* at the time of purchase.

Before and After

We had discussed the possible repercussions of changing a boat's name, but Masa put it aside as a ridiculous superstition and had the name changed to *Half Moon Bay*. She was a Skookum design built in Port Townsend, Washington. She was originally a fifty-three foot hull but the builder kicked her out another six feet adding the lazerette. The hull was fifty-nine feet on deck. With the bow sprit she lay sixty-five feet L.O.A. She had a seventy foot aluminum mast stepped onto the pilot house with roller furling jib and mainsail. The mast had a crows nest about half-way up. Above that was mounted the furuno, radar, and magnetron antenna which weighed fifty to sixty pounds. On the mast head were the lights, the VHF antenna and wind speed indicator which added more weight to the already heavy mast. I have seen nauseated people step off the boat onto the dock because she was top heavy and rolled so much. I believe this was her only defect. Apart from this she was about as sound as any boat on the seas.

The original owner had the boat rigged for fishing and research. He had chartered her out to research groups, as well as for his own use. After several years he returned to the mainland leaving the boat in Honolulu.

The boat was then leased several times. When Masa found her she was fairly trashed and homeless people were living aboard. He was able to buy her at a fair price. The only machinery in good shape and still functioning were the engines. Everything else was in need of repair. It was love at first sight. Valerie had once said that the *Half Moon Bay* was Masa's girlfriend. Masa had found his dream. He wanted to become a fisherman. I think that Masa's wanting to become a fisherman was a latent desire realized only after he had fulfilled his earlier sailing ambitions.

Masa loved this boat so much he started cleaning her before he knew his offer would be accepted. He told me the trash was knee high throughout the boat. I would go to Hawaii each year to work on the boat and to fish. Masa came to California to help me on the construction of my boat. We made a trip to Japan to work on his two boats which he was planning to sell in 1989.

The *Half Moon Bay* came equipped with all the required fishing permits along with the Mal Zone permit which included the outer islands toward Midway. At that time only about twenty boats had that permit and only about five boats were actively using it to bottom fish in that area. Although we had had our lessons, we were still beginners. Fishing Hawaiian waters is different than anywhere I have fished. Even the hooks used have an extra half turn to them. They looked as if it would be more difficult for a fish to take the hook. They worked surprisingly well. Whomever designed them knew what they were doing. Fishermen don't give away their secrets, but we were learning.

In 1990 I received a bonus. One of my dreams was to go commercial salmon fishing in Alaska. While growing up in Monterey, several of my classmates had been able to go fishing with their dads in Alaska. I would be green with envy. I met a guy in Hawaii who made a connection for me which allowed me and my son, Lance, to fish the salmon season in Alaska. My son wasn't too thrilled with the experience, but I loved every minute of it.

The season was a poor one for fishing. This gave me some unexpected free time and the opportunity to attend some AA meetings of which there were plenty. Summer with the unending daylight is work time for people in Alaska. It is not unusual for people to work 16 hour days and for fishermen to work around the clock. In contrast the long winter nights are mostly slack time, which can find a lot of people tipping the bottle. Consequently a lot of the local people were either found at the saloon or at AA meetings. Alaskans are like pioneers: strong and independent. On the whole, they're some of the friendliest people I've ever met.

May 1991: Masa was overseeing the construction of a sixty-five foot *McGregor* sailboat in Southern California for a buyer in Hokaido. I was in Hawaii waiting for his return. We flew to Japan to negotiate the sale of a Japanese fishing-training boat for a Cook Island corporation. The boat was destined for trade in the South Seas with Nancy Griffith as the skipper. When I first heard about the *Avatapu* I began to feel excited. It took me back to when I was a teenager. There had been a TV show called, "Adventures in Paradise". I think that this program was the source of my lifelong dream to go to sea and seek adventure. On the boat I'm building in California, I plan to have four to five hundred cubic feet of storage space specifically to carry goods for trade.

Nobuo first came to the *Half Moon Bay* while Masa was in Los Angeles. He had been sleeping in a camper shell and was looking for work. He appeared to be fairly thin. He told me that he did not want to return to Japan, that he wanted to make a life in America. I told him I would not let anyone stay on the boat without Masa's okay. I fed him and told him to come back when Masa had returned.

Masa talked with Nobuo and agreed to let him stay on the boat while we were in Japan. Masa was happy having someone on the *Half Moon Bay* because there were many undesirables hanging around Kewalo Basin. There were a lot of thefts and we were going to be gone for many weeks.

Masa and I flew to Tokyo and met John, the American engineer of the boat for which Masa was negotiating the sale. We traveled to Aioi on the south end of Honshu, after a brief stay at Masa's home in Kawasaki. In Aioi we began working on the *Avatapu*, the name chosen by the new owner. I gave her the name *Gomi Maru* and it stuck. The reason for name *Gomi Maru*, which in Japanese means "Garbage Boat", was because she was in such a mess. It got worse before it got better. She had been anchored in a small bay for twelve years.

Ten more people arrived from Honolulu three days later. We got down to some serious work including dry docking her which was quite an experience and education in itself. There is a considerable difference between dry docking and hulling out a sailboat. Hulling out a fiberglass boat usually consists of repairing blisters, replacing zinc shaft work and bottom paint. To dry dock a ship includes all of the work done to a fiberglass boat but on a greater scale. As the *Gomi Maru* was a steel boat, we also had to do some welding and patching.

For general repair work, a sailboat is first lifted out of the water with a crane. Two nylon straps are placed under her, setting her upon a cradle. A ship needing repair work is towed into a lock where the gate is closed. The water is pumped out and the ship is left sitting high and dry.

Avatapu in dry dock

We received word in late June that the sixty - five foot *McGregor* sail boat which Masa had been over-seeing the construction of in Southern California, was arriving in Yokohama. We would receive her in two days.

I was very anxious to leave the *Gomi Maru* and begin a new adventure. I knew I wouldn't be sailing on her maiden voyage. Living conditions were less than favorable. The water was foul and bathing was difficult. One of our water tanks had ruptured allowing diesel from the connecting fuel tank to enter. This wasn't detected until one night when Mary Doeffinger, one of the crew, was bathing. In the process of rinsing her shampooed hair she was drenched by diesel. I can still remember her screams. We gave her the nickname "Bilge Water Mary". Diesel, being lighter than water, floats on top of water. When the water ran out, the diesel flowed through the pipes. The highlight was when we got to go ashore to use the bathhouse. Japan still uses public bath houses. Now they're gender separate.

Damien Sailors, the boatswain, Robert Griffith, a deck hand and I officially earned the title of "Bilge Rats". While in dry dock, welding had to be done on the hull below the engine room. The dock workers wouldn't weld hull because our bilge was full of diesel and sludge. We had to drag sacks of cement across the ten bilge compartments which had barely enough room for a man to crawl through. The cement was then dumped in all the compartments and mixed with the fluid in the bilge. I doubted whether it would harden, but it did. The advantage of having done this was that the cement added ballast to the boat. I'm a firm believer in ballast. The more ballast the more stable the boat.

I spent a month on the *Gomi Maru*. It was uncomfortable. We had many inconveniences, but I have fond memories of the crew. Unfortunately, except for Masa and Robert Griffith, none of the original crew made the maiden voyage on *Avatapu* (the *Gomi Maru*). The crew arrived in Japan in June and, because of red tape, the boat didn't sail until December. For varying reasons the crew tired of waiting and drifted off in different directions, as most good sailors do.

It was a considerable distance from Aioi to Yokohama. We drove all day and arrived in Kawasaki in the wee hours. I had a lot of boat parts I had purchased from a boat salvage yard in Aioi where the *Gomi Maru* was anchored. I couldn't take them on our boat delivery to Hokaido. We arrived about 8 p.m. the next day in Yokohama. A launch then took us to where the *McGregor* was being lowered into the water by sling from the container ship which had brought the *McGregor* from Southern California. We boarded her. It took us a while to get her running because everything was poorly wired. We motored for about two hours to a marina where we would stay and which Masa had previously arranged. It took us several days to work out all the kinks and run her standing rigging, masts, radar, etc.

The sixty-five foot *McGregor* was nicely equipped. She had a V-8 Yammar auxiliary and two eight kilowatt generators, forced air and heat. She also had two full baths with showers, main salon and state room forward with a V-berth in the bow. The galley was a combination steering station with auto helm, chart table and radar. The captains quarters were aft of the galley, below the cockpit. Aft of the cockpit and through either of two small hatches was a small, cozy quarters large enough for two people. She was sloop rigged with a self-tending staysail. She would do twelve knots motor or sail in fair wind, quite fast for a production boat. What I liked about her was she was all plastic. Plastic requires minimal maintenance. Most boats have too much wood. Wood is very attractive, but requires a lot of work to keep it looking good. I think wood is not very practical for tropical cruising.

This was a fun trip with Masa as most were. The Japanese coast line consists mostly of small fishing villages. We would stop each night on the trip north up the eastern side of Honshu. Sailboats were uncommon on this side of Honshu. The local people would flock to the boat wherever we tied up. It was fun showing off the boat.

After several days we reached Hakodate on the southern tip of Hokaido. Hakodate is a sister city to San Francisco. She's built on steep hill sides in Victorian architecture and has marina restaurants along her water line like San Francisco. She had no trolley, but had a single cable car that journeys to a mountain peak above the city. Hakodate was the sight of the last civil war battle in Japan. The city was destroyed in 1907. When they rebuilt it, most of it was rebuilt in Victorian style. Masa told me this was because of the Dutch influence. It was a beautiful city and drew numerous tourists with its sidewalk vendors and antique shops.

Masa was always helpful about explaining the local customs and history of whatever island on which we landed. I gained a greater insight on the culture and their customs.

The next day the owner of the *McGregor* joined us in Hakodate. We set sail for Otaro City, the most northern port on the west side of Hokaido. We traveled west through the Tsugaru Straits then north up into the Sea of Japan.

The squid were running. It was a fascinating sight to see the thousands of squid boats at night. They have bright lights mounted all around the boats which shine into the water to attract the squid. This brings them to the surface where they're caught. I didn't ask Masa but I imagined the squid fishermen wore some sort of eye protection because of the brightness of the boat lights.

The Japanese take their fishing seriously; their boats are very fast. Japanese fishermen serve an apprenticeship just as carpenters do in America. The first time I saw the squid boats I didn't know what was happening. All these lights were scooting across the water so fast that they didn't look like boats. They were all juggling for position for fishing spots. At any time I could count a hundred boats around us. I was thankful that we had installed the radar because on the second night the fog moved in. It was so thick we couldn't see our own bow. Even with their bright lights, the squid boats were impossible to see until we were almost on top of them.

Otaro City is the most northern port on the west side of Hokkaido. You can look to the west and see Russia at a distance of only about fifteen miles across the water. I was told that summer in northern Hokaido is very short. Hot weather lasts only about three weeks. We had hit it just right; it must have reached seventy-five degrees in the daytime. The winters there are very harsh. Winds often blow down from Siberia; they call this the "Siberian Express". Masa told me they have a short crop season, growing mostly potatoes and corn.

The owner of the *McGregor* lived in Sapporo which was a short distance from Otaro City by train--maybe an hour. We stayed for several days with the owner. He was most hospitable and gracious. I reflected back to the Guam sail when Hidei, Takeo and I would lie around in the forecastle talking story. It was evident that they were proud of Honshu, their homeland. They told me about the different characteristics of the people from Hokkaido and Okinawa. I don't know about the southern island, but I saw no noticeable difference between people of Hokkaido and Honshu. Many people are proud of their homelands and think it's the "best place" to live in the country. At the time I felt the same way about California.

I flew from Sapporo to Tokyo and caught a train to Kawasaki. I had stored some port holes and boat lights there, which I had bought from the boat salvage yard in Aioi. I then flew to Honolulu, to check on the *Half Moon Bay* and to pick up the rest of my belongings, before continuing to California. Masa stayed in Hokkaido for a while longer to make some adjustments on the *McGregor*. I was anxious to get home and back to work on my boat.

Upon returning to California, I found myself getting a divorce from my wife and from a thirty-year marriage. Being gone six months at a time is not compatible for marriage. I found us growing in opposite directions. I had been spending too much time away from home the last four years. I could see the subtle changes occurring in our relationship. We were no longer the same people whom we had married. Everything around us is constantly changing. If we are healthy, we also grow and change. If not we stay the same and get left behind. The distance between us made it possible for me to see the tree in the forest. My wife had grown all the years I had stagnated. We were out of sync. She had developed her own line of supportive people in her quest of life, liberty and pursuit of happiness. She had many friends and activities, also her job to keep her occupied. None of her dreams or goals intersected with mine and likewise for me. Our children were grown. We felt there was no point in continuing our relationship as husband and wife. We had an amicable separation.

Except for the time when Lance developed a kidney disease (a form of glumerulo neuphritus) and had to go on dialysis (while I drowned my sorrow in alcohol), this was the hardest time of my life. I was now six years sober and drinking was no longer an option. For me to drink is to die. I still had dreams and things I wanted to do. There were times I wanted to run back to her bosom when the emotional pain became almost unbearable. I even thought about drinking--anything to make the pain go away. All that would do would be to postpone the pain. I've heard it said, "It's not how many times you fall but how many times you get up". I believe if you don't let divorce beat you, you come out a stronger person.

My brother, Michael, saw me suffering and said he knew how I could be free of my pain. All I had to do, he said, was get down on my knees, ask Jesus to be my personal savior, and ask Him to take the pain from me. I did and the Lord did take the pain from me. When this happened I knew I had found something in my life for which I had been searching.

I wandered around California and Oregon for a while then landed in Cave Junction, Oregon, at my other brother, Corky's. I was baptized in his church along with my nephew, Daniel, and I became a Christian reborn. For the first time in my life since I was in school, I began to know some peace of mind. I had always believed in the Holy Trinity, but I can't remember ever having asked Jesus to come into my life.

We raise our sons with the secret hope that they will fulfill our unfinished dreams. Either because of our own fears or misdirected choices, our dreams may be left unfulfilled. I don't know if my lust for adventure was a middle-aged whim to be young again, or a festering sore that had driven me since childhood.

When Lance was eighteen he visited Hawaii for a week. While there he made the decision to stay. This would not have been a problem except that he was on dialysis and was in a weakened state of health. He found a job, a place to live and began a new life. This made me very proud and somewhat ashamed of my own fears that develop from being a parent. That's when I decided that when I grow up I want to be just like Lance.

Raising Tiffany, without health problems, was more routine as raising children goes. She grew up to be a fairly happy and healthy child and young adult. She had good friends, all the things she needed as well as most of what she wanted. The most precious thing my daughter ever did was when she willingly and unselfishly gave one of her kidneys to her brother so that he could live a more normal life.

I started to buy a piece of land in Cave Junction. I soon realized I wouldn't be happy so far from the sea; I packed up and headed south. I landed in Ventura, California, where I bought a thirty-five foot center cockpit Coronado sloop. I hung around Ventura for a couple months prepping the *Ana Christine* for a cruise to Hawaii. I had wanted to single-hand to Hawaii for a long time and thought this a good opportunity.

The *Ana Christine* was fairly well equipped and had a 3 cylinder Yammar diesel auxiliary. I added a one cylinder Yammar diesel, two and a half kilowatt generator, a Raytheon radar and G.P.S. for cruising. She had a good inventory of sails, two reefing mains, a working jib, a one hundred thirty Genoa sail and a roller-furling jib. The only equipment she lacked was a storm jib. I liked her because she was all plastic and low maintenance. The only exterior wood on the *Ana Christine* was on her three hatches. At thirty-five feet she seemed as spacious as a *Peterson* forty-four sailboat. I especially liked the aft cabin which was basically all bed. It was very cozy with the TV and VCR. She was a comfortable live-aboard. Her only drawback was her displacement. She only weighed fifteen thousand pounds, not really heavy enough for a cruiser. In rough seas she would not be as stable as a heavier boat. But then again I haven't been on many boats that actually are stable in rough seas.

On July 11, 1992, I set sail for Hawaii. After sailing most of the day, I reached the island of Santa

Rosa in the Channel Island chain. This is where I learned my first lesson in buying a boat. Never buy a boat without having had it surveyed! I discovered I had a bent prop shaft. Sometimes when you buy something the seller doesn't lie to you; he just doesn't tell you everything. I discovered the bent shaft while motoring all night past Santa Rosa. The wind was blowing directly into my bow. I thought about turning back but decided to continue. In the morning, I would be clear of the island and in the open sea where I could set sail. I thought I would run South West past San Diego then West on the outside to avoid the shipping lane. After the scare near Fort Bragg in 1986, I didn't want to be anywhere near big ships. The winds were unfavorable. I could sail only North or South, and I was getting further South into Mexico than I wanted. I knew that there was a tropical depression heading my way from the South.

The second day I found myself still motoring. The wind was coming out of the west and blowing very light. The sun was beginning to set. I heard a spout blow off my port quarter, then to starboard and all around me. I got nervous. Louis Casey, a friend in Ventura, had told me a story of some people in Australia who had been sunk by a whale. I'd counted nine or ten whales when I suddenly remembered my prop was still spinning. I shifted

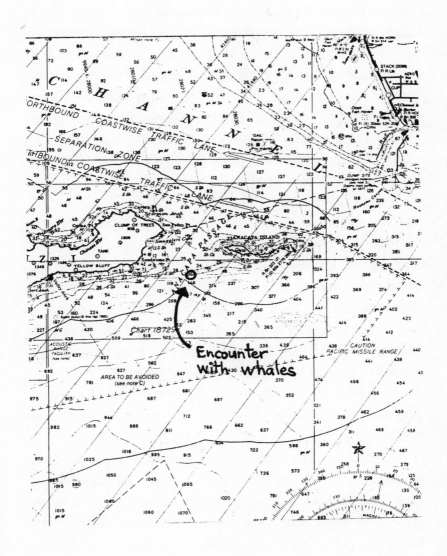

into neutral. All I could think of was what if a curious baby whale ran into my prop. Just a short time later I felt my boat lift and lean sideways several inches. Even though I was fearful I also felt a kinship with the whales. Although I'd seen many whales at first hand, this was the first time I was in the middle of a pod. This may sound ridiculous but I felt that the whale that had nestled my boat was not trying to do me harm, but to thank me for being considerate of the whales.

I felt awestruck to be sitting in the middle of a pod of whales and seeing them blow as they surfaced. I was also wondering if they were going to tear my boat apart. Then they all disappeared as quickly as they had come. Amazingly they did not even flap their tails out of water.

My roller-furling jib backlashed around my forestay and I couldn't free it. The main halyard fouled and I found myself with only a motor with the prop shaft beating against the through-hull. That was when I decided to head for San Diego to make repair.

I didn't have an auto helm. At night when I got tired I would pull down my sails and drift for a few hours while I slept. Not a recommended way to sail. This is also the way I managed to foul my main halyard.

One night I was awakened by my radar alarm. I looked to see what appeared to be a ship on my screen. It looked like it was circling me. I guess I was really tired. Having been awakened by the alarm was further disorienting. It took a couple minutes for me to figure out I was drifting in circles. When I went up to take a look, I got a heck of a surprise. I was in a fog but it was unlike the fog of the North Coast. This fog wasn't as dense and there was also the glow of the moon. The combination of the moon and my running lights made an eerie reflection. It looked like I was in the midst of many dumpsters with what appeared to be six story buildings all around me. There was no movement or sound. I felt like I was the only one left after World War III. I kept waiting to collide with something. After drifting for a while with all the images moving with me I began to understand that it was possibly an illusion.

I went below to scan the area with my radar. It showed nothing. I recalled having once been told to trust my instruments. This helped me feel better though I still felt very uneasy. I decided to never say anything to anyone about this experience.

When I'd left Ventura I figured I could run four or five hundred miles out by the time the storm came up the Coast. And that the storm would give fair winds to Hawaii. What I didn't count on was the El Ninos (warm water) coming up from Central America. Somehow the El Ninos affect the trades. Instead of a Southeaster or Northwester all I got was a light Westerly.

I motored at half speed North by Northeast for about twenty-four hours when I got hit. The storm from Mexico had caught me. I had calculated six days for the storm to come up the coast.

When the storm hit it was traveling due East; I decided to run with it. The sea was white with chop, but not high. I felt like I was in a runaway truck. The hull was humming and I was beginning to get nervous. I radioed the Coast Guard and told them what was happening. They advised me on procedures in case of a state of emergency where I would have to abandon ship. I put on my wet suit, tied my EPIRB onto my waist, went up into the cockpit and waited.

Suddenly the water changed from chop to a smooth deep trough. I was standing in the cockpit looking up at a wall of water about three feet over my head on both sides of my boat. The wind was traveling over the top; where I was it was reasonably calm. I had occasional splash, but if that wall of water had collapsed, I would have been in trouble. Previously I had cut back on my throttle leaving me only enough for steerage. Now it made no difference at all because I knew I could not traverse that wall of water. I maintained a slow speed letting the trough take me where it may. I felt helpless to do anything at this point.

I called the Coast Guard again to let them know my status. They asked if I could power out of the trough. I said I didn't know what was on the other side, if there was another trough or what. If I did manage to get out I would be stuck at the helm and unable to go below to radio them. They said they were in the area, would reach me in about three hours and to sit tight. They asked my position and course as I first entered the trough. My heading was due East but the wave was carrying me South. At the time I wasn't aware of my position and course. I believe I was in a mild state of panic. I had had very little sleep for five days and was suffering from nicotine withdrawal. I had thought this would be a good time to quit smoking. I believe if someone had come along at that time with a pack of Lucky Strikes I would have traded my boat for them.

The oddest thing then happened; the sea flattened. My boat made an abrupt ninety degree right turn and I was back in the trough heading due South. If I had been prepared I might have been able to turn to port and possibly pull out. It just happened too fast. This is when I became aware of my fear. I immediately called the Coast Guard and told them what had happened. The skipper asked my position and course and again said "sit tight". They were on their way. I guess he'd done some fast calculating and decided I wasn't where I should be according to my course and last reported position. A short time later he called back and asked if I had any physical problems. I was reluctant to tell him, but I thought it better that he knew I was legally blind.

There was a pause. He then asked if there was anyone I would like him to notify. Again I was reluctant because I wasn't expected to reach Hawaii for two to three more weeks. I could sense the suspicion in his voice. I felt that he wanted to contact someone to find out what kind of "nut" he was dealing with. I gave him my son's number in Los Angeles.

Shortly after the last call my boat made two more of those ninety degree turns. But these times the trough did not flatten. On the last turn, I saw my boat slide into a maelstrom deeper than the trough I'd been in. It was donut shaped with a spout in the middle. The spout and the outer wall looked to be about ten feet above my deck. It took over a minute to make one clockwise lap around the perimeter. It was like being in a hollow donut lying flat and cut in half. This is when I really got nervous. I thought for sure I was going to be swallowed up by the sea.

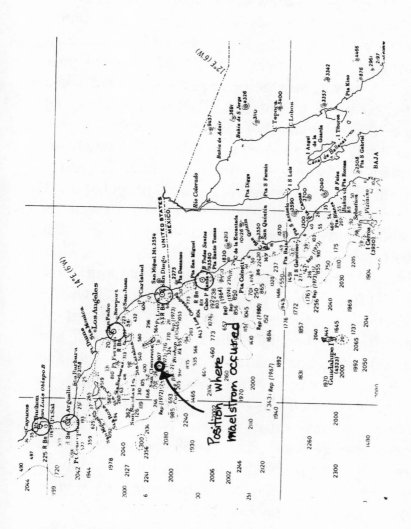

After a couple of hours the Coast Guard showed up. Some crew came down in a long boat, tied some lines to my bow and returned to the cutter. How they traversed the trough I couldn't see for it was a stormy, dark night. The Coast Guard skipper radioed to say he was going to pull me out and asked me to assist with my motor. When the slack was out of the towline I was bow up at forty five degrees. When I felt the tug I gave it full throttle. I could see the stern of the big Coast Guard cutter fishtailing back and forth above me. My bent propeller shaft was beating violently against the hull. This went on for about thirty seconds. It was obvious the cutter wasn't going to be able to pull me out. They released the tow line and I returned to circling in the donut. The skipper then called and asked what I wanted to do. My first thought was to go aboard the cutter, but the thought of losing the $30,000 I had invested in the boat made me think twice. I replied that I would like to save my boat. He said, "Sit tight till daylight" which was only a couple of hours away.

I must have dozed off because the next thing I remember there were three "Swabs" climbing on the deck. The trough had dissipated and it was blowing about fifty knots. They began defouling my rigging and got everything functioning properly.

I guess I must have looked pretty rough. After one of the crew conversed with his skipper, they decided to tow me in to San Diego. That suited me just fine. They took over the boat and I went below to the aft cabin which I hadn't slept in since I had left Ventura.

It was dusk when we docked at the Kettenburg dock on Shelter Island. The skipper of the Coast Guard cutter came aboard and pleasantly reamed me out. He strongly suggested that I not sail alone again. Also to notify him when I would sail out. I said I would. He added that I handled the experience about as well as anyone but implied, if I had good eye sight, I probably wouldn't have gotten in this fix. He was particularly unhappy about having to put his crew in harms way. I could only agree with him. He shook my hand and left. I turned to Lance and his wife, Kumiko, standing next to the boat. Lance smiled and asked how I was, then proceeded to laughingly tell me about the phone call. He said the skipper had asked if I was crazy. His reply was, "No, he's not crazy but, yes, he is crazy."

I believe a man has to make an attempt to pursue his dreams. If he doesn't he begins dying inside. It was one of my dreams to make a crossing single-handed. There comes a time when we have to acknowledge our limitations. Although I had thousands of cruising miles, I found I still needed a good pair of eyes with me. Steve Odehnal, a friend in Ventura, offered to sail with me to Hawaii. I thought that he would've been a good sailing companion but I really wanted to make this sail alone. I think that Molly, his wife, was quite relieved when he decided not to make the voyage with me. Even with a magnifying glass, I had a terrible time with my charts, not to mention the problems I had with my rigging. As I look back I'm happy that I did try even though I failed. At least I won't sit around when I'm old kicking myself for never having tried. Lance and Kumiko had to return to Los Angeles right away. I walked them to the parking lot, said good-bye and went to the nearest store for a pack of cigarettes.

The next day I hauled out. The machinist in the yard was very busy. I told him I was in no hurry because I was looking for crew. He could make my new prop shaft when he had the time. This gave me a chance to look around. I found San Diego very pretty, the people friendly. I ended up renting a slip at Shelter Island Marina. I moved there after making repairs and bottom paint.

While I was dry docked I was talking one day to one of the tow boat skippers. He had heard my conversation with the Coast Guard on his VHF. He told me he had never been in a maelstrom himself, but had heard about a fisherman in a small boat being caught in one. The fisherman had circled around picking up speed, he said, until he was able to break over the rim, a very gutsy move. I cautiously asked him about the off-shore fog and felt relieved when he described an experience similar to mine. He also said, "Trust your instruments".

I had never heard of a maelstrom. I guess the ocean is capable of just about anything. The only explanation I have for what happened to me is that possibly the warm current of the El Ninos traveling north had collided with the cooler Pacific current traveling South over shallow water and had created a whirlpool. The water was only sixty five fathoms where this incident occurred.

In August I met a guy who wanted to sail and we discussed sailing to Hawaii. He couldn't go until November. I thought that, instead of hanging around San Diego, I could go to Hawaii to fish and possibly make some money. I called Masa. He said we could fish through September, that he had to go to Japan in October. He was wanting to spend time with his elderly mother. He said, "Good timing". I bought a ticket for September 3rd for Hawaii.

I arrived in Honolulu about 1 p.m. I always travel light, with only what I can carry. I went directly to the baggage carousel exit. As I passed through the carousel room, I saw an Asian man sitting by himself and deep in thought. He was wearing a slouch hat and I couldn't see his face. I thought it could be Masa and paused for a few seconds in front of him. He didn't respond and I continued outside where I could smoke. I thought about how, in the first few minutes outside the airport, the Hawaiian air has a humid, pungent and tropical scent of foliage. Each time upon my arrival the fragrance lasts only a short time before I become accustomed to it. I was just about to reenter the airport when Masa came out. I could recognize his walk anywhere.

We drove directly to the *Half Moon Bay* while Masa filled me in on the last fourteen months. He told me that, after Hokaido, he had returned to Aioi and the *Gomi Maru*. Nobuo had joined him on the maiden voyage of the *Gomi Maru*. They had collected a lot of trade goods in Japan for trade in the south sea islands en route to the Cook Islands. The *Avatapu (Gomi Maru)* was purchased specifically for use as a trade ship. Nancy Griffith, the skipper, previously had had a large *ketch* she'd used for trading. That boat had run onto a reef and sank. Nancy was quite a sailor and co-authored a book with her husband Robert Griffith named "Blue Water."

Masa told me he had made some investments, but was financially strapped and currently operating on a shoestring. He said he had had one successful fishing trip, but was glad I was there because we would stay out fishing for as long as we wished. He had gone out with other skippers, but they all had other priorities. They couldn't stay out fishing as long as Masa wished.

Masa was a green card alien. He could own an American boat but could not fish American waters without an American skipper. (Jones Act).

When we reached the boat, I received less than a warm welcome from Nobuo. I was a bit puzzled at first, but as time passed, I saw him moving into my position. Masa had just passed the citizenship exam and now he and Valerie were sponsoring Nobuo. I guess Nobuo felt threatened by my presence, but that was okay with me. I don't think he understood that I was just there to fish. I'd be on the *Half Moon Bay* a short time; he had no reason to be threatened by me.

Nobuo was alot like me in that he too was looking for the excitement of life on the sea. He'd sailed with Masa on the maiden voyage of the *Avatapu*. Nobuo had a degree in marine biology but chose, at this time, to live the life of an adventurer. There is no better person for a sea gypsy to spend time with than Masa. Masa was Nubuo's mentor as he was mine.

Masa had given me an opportunity to become a partner, an offer which many men would give anything to have. I still wanted to be a sailor. There were a lot of islands out there I had not seen. Masa had seen them, his dream was now to be a fisherman. I didn't share his dream. I still longed for the unexplainable thrill of approaching an island where I've never been after days of sailing. Ever anxious to explore the island, to meet the native people and learn as much as I could about their customs and culture.

We spent the afternoon making leaders and preparing lures for our trip. After dinner we motored west for about an hour to catch bait fish. On each side of the storage hold and aft of the cabin were holds that could be used for storage or for fuel tanks. Masa was using them for live bait tanks. He had put pumps in them to keep the fish alive. Each one had about fifty fish in them. I guess they had been collecting bait fish nightly. It was about midnight when we tied up to the dock. Masa went home to Hawaii Kai; Nobuo and I stayed on the boat.

The next morning I stepped out on deck and noticed the pumps weren't working. All the fish were lying dead at the bottom of both tanks. I stepped inside and told Nobuo, but he acted as if it wasn't of any concern to him. When Masa arrived he was pissed. He didn't say much other than that we should have heard the pumps stop. On a boat one becomes accustomed to all sounds and is able to identify them. Being that I hadn't been on the boat for over a year and wasn't yet familiar with the sounds, I felt the responsibility to be Nobuo's.

The fuel truck arrived and we took on eight hundred gallons of diesel. We then moved across Kewalo Basin where we took on our crushed ice. They load the ice into a crusher on a truck. The truck pulls along side of the boat and pumps the crushed ice through a long, rubber hose, about one foot in diameter, into the fish hold.

Masa said he was going to take his car to Hawaii Kai and return on the bus; he would be gone awhile. When he left he told Nobuo to clean the tanks--a nasty job. I could tell this made Nobuo angry, but he didn't say anything. I've heard stories about whole crews dying because, either they lost their ice, or their refrigeration went out. The fumes from the rotting fish are so toxic it can kill you. When fish die it doesn't take long for them to spoil if they are not chilled immediately.

When Masa returned he greased the rudder box. We got under way approximately 8 p.m., Friday, September 4. We ran all night. The next morning we set out trolling lines and spent the day fishing around Niihau. We caught five or six ono and anchored at sundown. The next morning we lost our anchor after having fought with it for a couple hours. We reset our lines. This day proved to be less fruitful. At sundown we headed West all night for new fishing grounds.

The trolling was best in the morning and afternoon. During the middle of the day we would bottom fish. Our main bottom fish were opakapaka (red snapper) and budekari and several other species of bottom fish. We were doing quite well with a sizable catch everyday. We were maybe averaging five ono and a few tombo daily. Every night we would move to new grounds; this was working well.

On the 4th day the sun was breaking the horizon as Nobuo and I had just finished putting out our trolling lines. I felt Nobuo staring at me. I stopped and turned to see him standing on the stern at the end of the brine tank. I froze in my tracks when he pointed down to the brine tank and said, "Your coffin". I stood there dumfounded for a few seconds. I then replied, "No. More your size." I couldn't see the expression on his face. I didn't know if he was joking or being serious. I didn't find any humor in his statement.

I didn't know it at the time but those two words would ultimately save my life. I turned to the cabin to get a cup of coffee. I thought of Queequeg's coffin in the story Moby Dick and how it kept Ishmael alive. Then I let the idea go and thought about it no more.

This fourth day while we were fishing Masa made the statement, "I need fifty-six ono." I assume he chose that figure based on what he had earned on his previous trip. I thought this not unreasonable. We would, however, have to have an extremely good day if we didn't want to hold our fish too long a period by extending the length of our trip.

We continued fishing daytime and traveling at night. By the 6th day we were all getting tired. It's not that fishing was difficult; it was the constant rolling of the boat. It was continual work to try to maintain balance. This takes a lot of energy: taking a shower, trying to sit on the toilet, cooking, even trying to keep from rolling out of your rack when sleeping. The *Half Moon Bay* would roll thirty to forty-five degrees to each side in three to five seconds. If we had favorable wind we would put out our sails. This would stop our full roll. We would only roll half way or back to zero degrees. Yet using sails would add pitch to the motion. You had to have a good stomach on this boat. Even Masa would usually get a little sick on the first night. When this happened, he would look at me with disgust saying, "Normal people get sick." I would laugh. I never told him that sometimes my mouth got watery. Crackers always took care of the problem.

I don't think we were ever out more than ten days at one time. Yet I recall every trip on the way back to Honolulu feeling tired and thinking, "I'm going to sleep for three days." Because of the constant motion of the boat, we were never able to get a restful sleep. The lack of sleep, inevitably, would take its toll on us. I would always lose at least ten pounds on each trip, but would gain it back just as quickly.

One night, a couple years prior to *Iniki*, Masa and I were out on one of our many unsuccessful fishing trips. It was unusually rough. We had our sails up. I was on watch about 1 am; Masa was asleep down below. We had a preventer on the boom which was slapping against the side of the cabin. I didn't want to go outside, water was coming over the gunnels. I had taken a shower two hours earlier and didn't feel like getting salty again. I listened to the slapping for a few more minutes and knew I couldn't stand it any more. I stepped outside.

When the *Half Moon Bay* rolls, you time your steps as you walk across the deck. You move across as the deck comes up toward you. After I stepped out the door, I moved directly to the capstan. I then planned to move around the ice maker, along the gunnel and forward to amidships where the preventer was tied. She was half-rolling rather quickly. I timed it and moved. This was my intention. I took two steps, she rolled back and I was in a no gravity dive with no deck under my feet. I reached out with my left hand, grabbed the side rail of the ice maker. My momentum carried me around to where I was able to grab hold with my right hand. I flagged out over the water for several seconds before the boat came up and I was able to plant my feet. Heart pounding, I edged my way very carefully along the gunnel, adjusted the preventer and made my way back into the cabin.

I have a saying that a cowboy knows his ride is over in eight seconds. On the *Half Moon Bay* your ride wasn't over until she was tied to the dock. I never did sleep for three days after a trip. Inevitably, the next day, I forgot about being tired. I was always eager to go again. I guess that was because of the excitement I felt while being at sea.

On the 5th day we were bottom fishing; I was having a bad day. I managed to lose four setups and could tell that Masa was getting irritated even though he didn't say anything. Masa had a Buck knife which Valerie had given him; he kept it very sharp. Nobuo had been using it to cut squid for bait. Later I saw Nobuo go to the galley and get another knife.

Late that evening I was sitting at the table when Masa sat down across from me. He said, "Losing gear is one thing but the knife was personal and it was a gift." After the way my day had gone I could understand how he could think this though he never asked me if I had lost his knife. It looked as if

Nobuo had laid it off on me. I felt that a who-done-it argument would be futile at this point so I didn't say anything. I just nodded my head. I felt angry but decided not to press the point. Aboard ship is no place for confrontations. I made a mental note that I would discuss this with Nobuo after the trip ended.

The sixth and last day we fished. The sun was hardly above the horizon when things started popping. Up to this point we had caught thirty-five ono. Our ice was getting low. At noon we had just caught fifty-six ono and we were completely out of ice. We didn't have any ice for our brine tank.

This is where the "what ifs" come in. I had the authority as legal skipper of the boat to call it a day. If we had left at this time could we have made it out of harm's way or even to Honolulu? I didn't know Masa's true financial situation. I knew his biggest complaint was that he wanted to stay till he was ready to head for the barn. My concern was, how were we going to handle anymore fish. I didn't want to bump heads with Masa because I figured we could get in a couple more trips by the end of the month.

Then things got crazy. The ono were hitting on all lines as were the sharks. For every four ono we hooked we might pull in one. Most of the time we landed heads while the sharks took the bodies. The shark bite was so clean the ono looked as if they'd been cut with a filet knife. Blood was rolling off the deck; we didn't have time to wash. We usually washed the deck after each fish was caught. We had to cut their jugglers to bleed them as this improves the taste of the fish.

We snagged a shark and pulled him in. I couldn't see what kind of shark it was because I only saw the underside. The lure hung in his bottom teeth, his head was out of water with his mouth wide open. Masa said, "Hold him". He got the shotgun and killed it. I thought about cutting the line when Masa went for the gun. It wouldn't make any difference to kill this one as it wasn't the only shark around us. They were all over the place. I started to feel sick inside. I don't know if Masa's blood was boiling from the thrill of the kill, or if he was angry about all the fish we'd lost because of the sharks. I thought it wasteful to continue fishing at this time. All we were doing was feeding the sharks.

I don't know why but, once again, I thought of Moby Dick. Although Captain Ahab was driven by revenge I somehow equated the two: revenge and Masa's drive to catch all the fish he could. Under my breath I asked God to make the fish stop biting. I didn't have the guts to ask Masa to stop fishing.

The bite continued until sundown. For all the fish we hooked we netted only fourteen more. Now what to do with the fish? Although our hold was refrigerated we could not bring the temperature of the fish down fast because we did not have ice for the brine tank. Consequently this would make their eyes cloudy. They wouldn't look as fresh at the auction. All we had on board was carpet to separate them. If the fish moved, their pretty, silver color would rub off their skin. Ono don't have scales like bottom fish. Masa knew these were things the buyers looked for at the auction. A few bad fish could bring down the entire price of the whole catch. Masa was aware of all this.

It was dark when we climbed out of the fish hold and got everything washed down. I started to leave the brine tank unwashed. Something kept nagging at me to wash it out which I then did.

In the Sea

One p.m., September eleventh: The sea was getting very high again. I was about one hundred feet off the bow of the *Half Moon Bay*. The wind and current were carrying me away from the boat, when I heard Masa yell, "Bob"! I looked and all I could see of the boat was the top of the pilot house and the mast. Masa and Nobuo were standing on top of the deck holding onto the shrouds and mast. Masa beckoned with a motion of his arm. He and Nobuo disappeared in the waves for about a minute. I knew there were only two life jackets, that if I left the tank I would have nothing to hang onto. I knew the boat would soon be gone.

Rule of thumb is, you stay with the boat until it's gone. I couldn't see any reason to go back. I knew I couldn't maneuver the tank back without exhausting myself. I also knew I had to conserve my strength. The Coast Guard doesn't send choppers out in a hurricane nor do they search at night. At the very least I would be in the water until the next day. Once again, I thought of Queequeg's coffin and how it kept Ishmael alive for one day and one night in the story of Moby Dick. I knew the brine tank was my salvation. I saw Masa and Nobuo and the top of the boat once more, but only long enough to wave good-bye. I only knew that to return to the boat would be folly and even death. I never saw them again.

I was already cramping from dehydration. First my toes curled under but, when I bent my legs so I could reach them, the back of my legs cramped. Then the fronts of my legs cramped when I tried to straighten them. I was in a lot of pain but I knew if I wanted to survive I had to relax. This was a major challenge because I was getting chilled. I was shivering and my teeth started chattering. I figured the only way to get warm was to kick my legs.

I don't know how I did it but I managed to block out the pain, relax and kick my feet at the same time. The seas started breaking over me now. I was traveling with the storm with the wind at my back. It was easy to keep the tank in front of me. This was good because the horizontal wind-blown water was hitting me in the back of the head instead of my face. I was getting blasted pretty good and the back of my head was numb. I reached back one time to see if I still had hair. It's hard to describe what water traveling in winds in excess of one hundred sixty-five knots feels like on the back of your head. Anytime I was high on a wave I would try to stay as low in the water as possible to keep from being pelted by the horizontal water.

The bad part was when I would get pounded under. Waves thirty to forty feet would lurch over from behind. I wouldn't see them until I was in the curl. I would have just enough time to grab a gulp of air and push myself clear of the tank. Then I would be deep under water, kicking and fighting to get to the surface. The first few times when I reached the surface I felt panicky. The surface had about six to eight inches of white foam and the tank was white making it difficult for me to find. Being a weak swimmer I knew if I lost the tank, I was a goner.

Being alone out here was like being in hell without dying. Except for God, no one knew I was out here. I believe the loneliness was more terrifying than all the tribulations I had to endure. I came to the understanding that I was in deep trouble and I wasn't going to make it by myself. I looked up at the dark sky and started to yell to the Lord. This was the first time I heard the roar of the storm. The wind just drowned my voice. The storm was deafening and I hadn't even heard it.

I remember playing high school football. In the heat of battle while struggling with the opponent, adrenaline flowing, I would have total concentration on the goal. Until the goal line was reached I saw, smelled and felt. But the only sounds I heard were those pertaining to the task at hand. The second the goal was acquired I could hear everything again. Like the flip of a switch, I could hear the crowd. I hold this likeness to the concentration of survival. I didn't hear the roaring engine inside the boat, the crashing sea or the raging wind, only my thoughts and Masa's words.

I thought about it for a second and I knew He would hear me. I looked up and in a slightly higher than normal voice I said, "Lord if it be your will, get me out of this. If you do I will become a fisher of men instead of a fisherman." From that moment on I knew I would make it yet I knew it was not going to be easy.

Then I got a break. I discovered four strands of tough string which had held to one of the eyes located on the middle of the tank. They were only about a foot long and too small to grip. They just pulled out of my hand, but I was able to lock them with one wrap around my finger. From then on when I was pounded under I stayed in contact with the tank.

I knew my body needed salt and it needed water. The most practical thing to do was to drink salt water. I had heard many things about people drinking sea water including the idea that it would make you mad. I figured I had nothing to lose and occasionally would take a sip or two in long intervals. After a couple hours I began to urinate. The cramping in my limbs had lessened. I realized my body was acting like a sponge. It was absorbing the fluid it needed because I hadn't drank that much. I stopped drinking the sea water. Besides it didn't taste good.

I saw debris float past me including a six-pack of sliced peaches which I started to grab when I realized I had no way to open the cans. The two Tupperware bowls that we kept our cut bait in when we were fishing came floating by. I grabbed them and put them under the tank thinking I might be able to catch rain water in the bowls. The next time I got knocked under they disappeared.

I remembered Nobuo throwing the bowls into the storage hold earlier. The hatch from the storage hold was four foot by four foot and weighed fifty or sixty pounds. It had a latch at each corner which a wrench or socket could turn. I assumed this compartment was water tight because the hold had sometimes been used to haul extra fuel on long trips. If we had thought to secure it could the boat have stayed afloat?

Every once in a while I would feel something next to my legs and feet while kicking. From fear of what I might see I wouldn't look back, or down into the water.

I started calculating whether I had the stamina to kick my legs through to the next day. I recalled how, when I used to work on the docks, I would sometimes work thirty-six hours on my feet loading freight by hand. It had been a few years since I had done that kind of work. However, for the last seven years, I've been jumping rope and walking daily; I have good endurance.

In comparison to what I was doing to survive, I equated it to a twenty-four hour hike. When I thought of it in those terms, it didn't seem like such a big obstacle. I was urinating about once an hour five or six times, then the intervals became longer. I think my system was stabilizing. I started playing with numbers in my head to pass the time, but I found myself separating from the tank. I realized it was going to take total concentration, that I had to stay focused on relaxing, kicking my legs and hanging onto the tank.

As it started getting dark I noticed the sea was calming. It dawned on me that I hadn't been knocked under for awhile. The waves had stopped breaking and the wind was diminishing.

The night air was colder than the water. I had to try to keep my shoulders under water. This required changing my position by holding the tank further away from my body. I had to kick more frequently to stay warm. I thought that, if I had a life jacket on, it would have held me up exposing me to the cold air. The water temperature was seventy degrees, almost thirty degrees below body temperature. I knew my body temperature had to drop only a few degrees and I was finished.

I began craving a cigarette. I thought, "You're on the brink of death and you're wanting a cigarette--idiot!" Then the craving passed and I thought of it no more.

It was dark now and I could see the lights of Kauai. There weren't many lights because the storm had knocked out the power on the island. I was on the southwest side of the island drifting northwest at about one mile per hour, approximately five miles off shore. I made a conscious effort to try to reach the island. Even though I knew I couldn't maneuver the tank that far, it gave me a purpose or goal to work for.

September 11th was a full moon. When I saw it rise from behind the island, I knew it would have to complete its arc before daylight would come and the glorious sun with it. All I could think about was getting warm. I knew I would probably blister, but I didn't care as long as I was warm.

I thought about leaving the tank and swimming for shore, but I quickly dismissed that idea. I'm not a buoyant person and have never been a good swimmer. As cramped as I was, I doubted if I could make it a hundred yards. The thought of losing my tank was scary. Another concern: If I were a strong swimmer and opted to try to swim to shore, I didn't know what the coastline was like. I could've been ripped to shreds by the coral or rocks onshore.

The moon was about halfway on its downward arc when I began hallucinating. I imagined a sailboat anchored to my right with a woman around forty years old wanting to give me some clothes, but her father said no. I then dreamed someone was trying to hand me a T-shirt, but I knew I couldn't let go of the tank to put on the shirt. I imagined that someone had built a porch on a shallow reef off to my left so I could stand on it to put on the T-shirt. I guess the significance of the hallucination was that it was ingrained in my subconscious that I couldn't let go of the tank.

Sometimes during the night after I began hallucinating, I became aware that I was weakening. Although I had always been a physically strong person, I'd never considered myself mentally tough. As I look back, I believe that it became more of a mental than physical battle to stay focused and determined to hold onto the tank.

Then I saw the fin. It was so close I could've reached out and touched it. It cruised slowly along my right side up around the end of the tank and back to my left side. It then disappeared under water. I don't know how long it had been in the area or if it was what I had felt around my legs during the day and night. I shook my head and said, "You're just dreaming."

I had several open wounds. I had a gash on my left hand. All the tissue down to the tendons was worn off my right ring finger. I had some gashes around my ankles. The wounds on my ankles were caused by my stupidity. The day before I had been wearing levis tucked into my foul weather boots with no socks. My legs had gotten wet from the water and blood from the fish. I could feel the hems of my levis gnawing at my ankles, but we were busy fishing all day. I wouldn't take the time to do anything about it. I knew the sharks could smell my blood. The kicking of my legs would also attract them. I also knew that my first priority was to stay warm. I told myself, "I can't worry about sharks." I put it out of my mind. I can't deny that I was afraid. I believe my emotions were shutting down. The entire experience was one whole frightening ordeal. Staying alive was my goal. I simply had to put first things first: holding onto the tank and keeping as warm as I could by kicking my legs.

I've often wondered if sharks can smell fear like dogs and other animals can. I knew that panic would only get me killed.

Finally the sky started to lighten. I was extremely cold and tired. The trades had returned and there was a mild breeze blowing. The sea had become about a two foot chop. This was very annoying. My eyes were on fire from the salt. The daylight added to the irritation. It was futile to wipe my face because my hands were wet. It only irritated my eyes more. They felt raw--like I had sand it them. It even hurt to blink.

Once again doubt and that maddening loneliness began to set it. The sky was cloudy, there was no sun. It was still as cold as it had been during the night. I could no longer see the island. Without the sun I couldn't tell the direction I was drifting. I became disoriented. Yet it didn't seem to even matter. I was helpless to do anything about it anyway. Previously I had felt some sense of consolation in knowing which way I was going. I'd been reasonably sure I was drifting west with the current and out to sea.

I dropped off to sleep once during the night with my chin resting on the tank, but was awakened by a wave slapping me across the face. I knew I was extremely exhausted. The second and last time I fell asleep I slipped under and came up spitting and gagging water. This scared away the sleep that had been hounding me.

My heart jumped when I heard a helicopter overhead. It was above the cloud cover and traveling fast. I thought it was traveling west. I wondered why they would fly so high if they were searching. About twenty minutes later I heard it again heading in the opposite direction. And again, it was too high to see.

I then became filled with despair. My legs, where they attach to my torso, were cramping. I couldn't lay out to kick my legs anymore. I was doubled up at ninety degrees. It was becoming increasingly painful to kick my legs. I calculated then that, at best, I had maybe one hour left. I understand that, when hypothermia sets in, the mind is still alert but that you lose control of your limbs. I never thought about drowning. Better to have a shark hit me, I thought, and bleed to death.

Shortly, maybe half hour later, I heard the chopper above and behind me to my left about four hundred feet. I knew they could see the tank because it was white and the sea was dark. All the foam had dissipated. I didn't know if they could see my dark body. I pulled the white tank under my torso so they could see my outline, and waved my left arm. I started to yell, but realized there was no way they could hear me. I then resumed my old

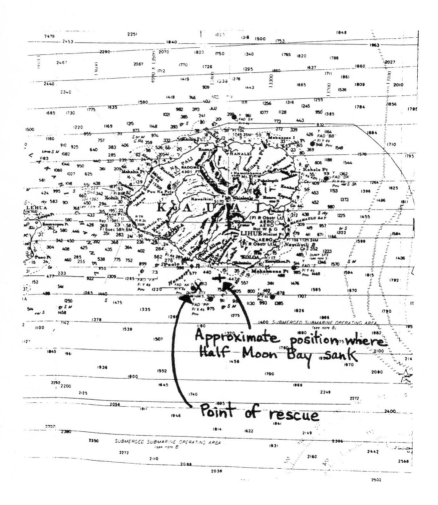

Approximate position where
Half-Moon Bay sank

Point of rescue

position. I watched as they lowered the basket. It was about fifty feet away. I thought about swimming toward it, but I knew I wouldn't make it. I turned my head back toward the tank as a sign that I couldn't let go of the tank.

A minute later, Patrick Estrada, the rescue diver from the Coast Guard helicopter, was next to me in the water. He asked if I was alright. I said, "Yes, but I can't swim". He slipped a life jacket over my head, cinched up the straps and said, "Relax". I had no problem with that. Then he pulled me to the basket. I wondered why they didn't put the basket next to me.

This was the first time in twenty four hours I felt safe. Much of the feeling of safety was just being with and hearing another human voice. That awful feeling of loneliness was gone. Dan Barber, the technician operating the basket, brought me up then retrieved Estrada. Meanwhile Larry Cheeks, the pilot and his co-pilot, John Church, had turned and headed the helicopter toward Kauai. As soon as the diver was aboard he grabbed a wool blanket and wrapped it around me. I was still shivering. Estrada took another blanket and wrapped that around me also. The high-pitched noise in the chopper was deafening. I held my hands over my ears until he handed me some ear covers. Then I curled up in the blankets. I immediately started warming up and was surprised that my body could still create heat. I felt like I was back in my mother's womb.

I was only in the chopper maybe ten minutes when we landed at Waimea Veterans Hospital on Kauai. When we were clear of the chopper, and they were wheeling me in on a gurney, I asked Estrada, who had attended me if they had picked up my partners. He replied no, but that they were still looking. I realized I hadn't thought about Masa and Nobuo since I had waved good-bye to them. I also knew they were dead.

Death is at all times solemn, but never so much so as at sea. A man dies on shore; his body remains with his friends, and "the mourners go about the streets"; but when a man falls overboard at sea and is lost, there is a suddenness in the event, and a difficulty in realizing it, which give to it an air of awful mystery...at sea, the man is near you--at your side--you hear his voice, and in an instant he is gone, and nothing but the vacancy shows his loss". ("Two Years Before The Mast" by Richard Henry Dana, page 77, paragraph 2).

Masa and Nobuo were slight of build and neither had the muscle or fat tissue to protect them from the cold. Even if they had been with me and had done what I did, I doubt if they could have endured the cold or had the stamina to hold on for twenty hours.

I don't know what became of Masa and Nobuo. They were never found. I only hope it was fast and painless. I've always believed that we all have an appointment with death. It doesn't matter which path we choose to take in life. We will ultimately be at the designated place and time.

The doctors and nurses at the hospital had been working around the clock since the hurricane had struck. There was little water. The hospital electricity was from their back-up generator. Many of the hospital staff had lost their homes and did not know where they and their families were going to live. Yet they maintained a professional attitude. The patients came first. I felt a genuine loving care from the staff and people of Kauai.

I weathered the storm surprisingly well. The only problem was an infection in my eyes. With antibiotic drops it cleared up in a few days. The water supply was still a dribble. I wasn't able to wash off the salt until the second day.

My daughter on Oahu heard I had been picked up and taken to Waimea Veterans Hospital, but didn't know my condition. She called KSSK, a local radio station on Oahu, and asked if they could broadcast for a ham radio to relay my condition. Oahu-Kauai communication was dead. The announcer was impressed with the story and put her live on the radio.

Gladys Okata, who lives on the hill above Waimea Hospital, was out raking debris from her yard when she heard the broadcast from KSSK on her portable radio. She stopped what she was doing and came to my side to see if she could be of any assistance. She spoke with me for a while, surveyed my situation and relayed my daughter's message. Mrs. Okata then prayed with me and my hospital roommate, Tom Tanaka. Tom was suffering from pancreatic cancer. I experienced Tom as being a gentle and caring person. Unfortunately he died a few months later.

Ohana (family). I had never heard that Hawaiian word. I learned the meaning that day. I had lost all my clothes, my passport, all my identification and, most important, my automatic teller machine (ATM) card by which I live. The only thing I possessed were the cut-off sweat pants I had on when I was pulled from the water. This kind lady, Mrs. Okata, brought me a goody bag. It included tooth brush, tooth paste, goodies to eat, shorts, shirt and a beautiful little book about giving and love. There was a card that read, "Humbly accept this gift". Inside the card was some cash. This came in very handy for the essentials I needed until I could replace my ATM card. One of the male nurses had an old pair of deck shoes he gave me. My outfit was complete.

KSSK later interviewed me live on the radio a couple of times. They said that if I wanted a copy of the interviews to stop by the station. I told the announcer about Mrs. Okata, who had come to see me at the hospital. He said he had heard of her and of her many good deeds. I shall never forget her or her kindness.

They say that "everyone has his or her three minutes of fame." I caught mine Sunday evening. Robert Hager from NBC, and his camera crew, came into my room and interviewed me for national television.

I had heard the storm did some damage on Oahu. My mind was put to ease to know that my daughter and her family were okay. She didn't learn of my physical condition until I returned to Oahu. She had never received a response to her broadcast.

On my ride from Waimea to Lihue, I was shocked at the devastation I saw. Debris was everywhere. It looked like a war zone to me. Trees were uprooted, telephone poles were broken, wires were laying in the streets. Sugar cane fields looked like cooked spaghetti. You couldn't see a single leaf on tree or bush. Every other house had lost its roof. One two-story house stands out in my memory. The inner and outer walls and roof were gone. The frame was intact along with the furniture. The sight was so pathetic yet I couldn't help but chuckle. It seems amazing that only three people were killed on the island during Hurricane Iniki. To have a force six storm hit an area where houses are lightly constructed and to not have hundreds of people killed was a miracle.

When I arrived at the airport, I was astonished at the number of tourists being evacuated. Later I heard that there were approximately ten thousand visitors on the island when Iniki struck. The local population and the authorities were anxious for the tourists to leave because of the shortage of food and fresh water on the island. Most of the evacuation was done by military transport and Hawaiian Airlines who donated planes and fuel for the evacuation.

I was recuperating at my daughter's home in Kapolei Oahu. I felt happy to be alive after being so close to a watery grave. The reality hit home when my daughter talked with a lady who was traveling to Kauai with the Red Cross. She had met the pilot of the rescue helicopter, Lt. Com. Larry Cheek. He had said, "If you see him tell him he is one lucky guy." They had run all their search patterns when they located the damaged EPIRB which was sending off a weak signal. The crew had said, "All pau (finished). Let's go in." But the pilot said, "I want to check the debris one more time. Besides we have enough fuel to run one more sortey." That's when they found me.

I spoke later with Dave Davies, fisherman and boat builder, at Kewalo Basin. I had told him that we had left on Friday, September 4th. He informed me that fishermen consider it bad luck to leave for a fishing trip on a Friday. They leave one minute before midnight Thursday, or one minute after midnight on Saturday, but never on Friday. We were still amateurs and hadn't known all the rules.

I understand that I crammed a lifetime of adventure into seven years. The brief time I knew Masa was the most exciting time of my life. He was always on the move with a new adventure each day. I learned early not to press him for details about what was to come. I think he derived pleasure from the surprises he gave me.

I got a little too close to the edge a couple of times and have learned not to push too hard. As a result of this, my life has slowed considerably. Maybe I'm beginning to grow up. Since *Iniki* my vision has further deteriorated. My left eye is 20/1000 and right is 20/500 with no night vision. This means if and when I sail again I'll be going on as passenger.

When I first became sober I thought my life was over. That it was going to be drudgery and boredom from here on out. At fifteen months of sobriety I began to think that, when I'm in my rocking chair, I won't have any stories to tell my grandchildren. I believe that If God is willing there aren't any obstacles we can't overcome in order to fulfill our dreams.

The AA Medallion awarded every year for continual sobriety has a Roman numeral for the amount of years a member has continuous sobriety. Inscribed on the medallion is the slogan, "To Thine Own Self Be True." Through my first seven years I pondered the meaning of this. My experience with *Iniki* reduced me to my smallest fiber. I learned who I am and of what I am made. It humbled me to know how insignificant I am. Before I could be honest with myself I had to discover who I am. The most important thing I learned was that "except for God, nothing matters." That left me with an inner peace for which I had been searching most of my life.

Today when the world starts to get heavy and things begin to close in on me, all I have to do is imagine myself back in the sea with Hurricane *Iniki*. Striving to become a better person is a full-time job. It requires continual surveillance over my behavior and character defects while keeping my ego in check.

GLOSSARY OF NAUTICAL TERMS

BULKHEAD Wall or partition on a boat.

CAPSTAN A machine placed perpendicularly in the deck, and used for a strong purchase in heaving or hoisting such as anchor or net.

FORECASTLE A foreward section before the mast where the sailors' quarters are located.

GENOA A large overlappying headsail set in light to fair winds.

GUNNEL (old spelling Gunwale) Lower walls along outside deck.

JIB (or Foresail) The foremost sail of a ship, triangular in shape.

L.O.A. Length overall.

MAIN SHROUD Cable or line to hold standing rigging such as mast.

PAINTER A line used to fasten a boat to a ship or other object.

PORT The left side of a boat facing forward.

SCUPPER A channel or gutter at the outer edge of the deck of a boat for carrying off water.

STANCHION Upright supports for lifelines around perimeter of boat.

STARBOARD Right side of boat.

STAY Provided support for the standing rigging as in forestay.

STAYSAIL Sail set on stay forward of the mast and aft of foresail.

WINDLASS A hoisting or hauling apparatus, operated mechanically or by hand, consisting of a horizontal barrel or drum on which is wound the rope or chain attached to the object to be raised or moved, usually an anchor.